Desmond O

THE COMPL

OF

THE WHOLE WORLD

Henry V
(as portrayed by the author)

Patrick Barlow

THE COMPLETE HISTORY
OF THE
WHOLE WORLD
or
From Amoeba to Cosmonaut

by

DESMOND OLIVIER DINGLE

Artistic Director
The National Theatre of Brent

assisted by
Raymond Box

Sumptuously illustrated by the Author

Exclusive Foreword by
Simon Schama

London
NICK HERN BOOKS
www.nickhernbooks.co.uk

A Nick Hern Book

Desmond Dingle's
The Complete History of the Whole World
was first published in Great Britain in 2002
as a paperback original by Nick Hern Books Ltd
14 Larden Road, London W3 7ST.

British Library Cataloguing data for this book
is available from the British Library

ISBN 1 85459 662 4

Cover design: Ned Hoste, 2H

Front cover photograph and others of
the author (and assistant) in historical uniform
by Mike Smallcombe

Typeset by Country Setting
Kingsdown, Kent CT14 8ES

Printed and bound in Great Britain
by Biddles, Guildford

For Nell

Other Works
by
Desmond Olivier Dingle

SO YOU WANT TO ACT?

MY LIFE IN ART
by Desmond Dingle

THE COMPLETE HISTORY OF THE WHOLE WORLD
for the young

THE COMPLETE HISTORY OF THE WHOLE WORLD
for the elderly

THE COMPLETE HISTORY OF THE WHOLE WORLD
pop-up version

DESMOND DINGLE'S DIARIES

DESMOND DINGLE'S I CHING

HOW TO WRITE FOR THE WEST END
by Desmond Dingle

DESMOND DINGLE'S
ENCYCLOPEDIA OF WORLD KNOWLEDGE
(twelve volumes)

*all the above soon to be published
by Nick Hern Books Ltd*

Foreword
by
Simon Schama

Simon Schama
New York

13 August 2001

Dear Mr Dingle,

Yes, I did receive another copy of your book 'The Complete History of the Whole World'.

As I said in my last letter I have tried to read it but find it almost impossible to understand. As such I'm afraid I really cannot write the foreword that you request. I am sure you will understand that I can only really endorse a work which dramatically extends the boundaries of human knowledge.

To be honest, I would be rather surprised if your second choice of Lady Antonia Fraser is 'in the bag' as you suggest. But then I could be wrong.

I am returning your cheque for £25.

Yours sincerely,

P.S. Please get off my back.

Contents

List of Plates

Dedicated

to my mother

MRS EVADNE DINGLE

'There's no tomorrow to a willing mind.'

(Lady Winchelsea)

Preface

WHEN I was a small boy, lying under the open window above my bedhead, there was nothing I liked better than to hear stories told to me by my father, the world-famous explorer Ronald Dingle. These tended to be somewhat rare occurrences seeing as he was often away for long stretches of fifteen or twenty-five years, sometimes concurrently.

But as I lay listening to those mighty tales of worlds gone by, I dreamt that one day, when I too became a man and took up manly pursuits and he was long gone (which he has been now for quite a time, as it happens, seeing as he went on a long journey to Rio de Janeiro from whence he did not return) that I might tell those tales again to new generations beneath the same stars.

And so it is that I have been graced with just that privilege, given to me by my public, not to mention Nick Herm Books, who saw within me 'a flame no other man could see'.

And so, without further ado, I take up my pen. And bend myself before this mighty task in hand to tell the history of the *whole* Universe from before it was begun to the present.

So sit back now and see unfold the days gone by until today, so that we may truly understand tomorrow.

Thank you.

DESMOND OLIVIER DINGLE

Dollis Hill, 2001

Second Preface

THE history of the human race is one of the most fascinating stories the world has ever known. Who would have thought, back in the petrified rain forests full of prehistoric monkeys where now stand modern cities such as Southampton and Leeds, that all them monkeys would one day evolve into human kind of the ilk of Scott of the Antarctic or George Bush. Not even major historians such as Lady Antonia Fraser or Simon Schrama when they was prehistoric monkeys could have foretold such a future.

In the same fascinating and yet remarkable way, my own career has bloomed with uncanny similarity.

For who would have thought that one day I myself would become not only renowned throughout the world as Artistic Director of the National Theatre of Brent – probably one of the most loved national theatre companies in the kingdom – but also an authority on the astounding number of subjects I am in fact an authority on.

For I too – like a shooting star – has leapt from humble origins to stardom in a mere moment. In fact, when you come to think about it and without wishing to blow my own trumpet obviously, it is as if I, Desmond Olivier Dingle, can become mankind himself.

And so – without further ado – let us embark upon the great highway of history towards that destination which we know not what and of which we are but the ancestors.

DESMOND OLIVIER DINGLE

Dollis Hill, 2001

Third Preface

FINALLY, I should just like to acknowledge my gratitude to Mrs Doreen Wheatley for the kind loan of her felt-tips and, in conclusion, the entire acting company of the National Theatre of Brent – and my trainee and assistant Raymond Box who, because I generously permitted him to feature in a number of historic poses within this volume, has seen fit to pass comment on the ensuing contents whenever he feels like it. All such comments should be ignored. Thank you.

DESMOND OLIVIER DINGLE

Dollis Hill, 2001

THE COMPLETE HISTORY
OF
THE WHOLE WORLD

CHAPTER I

The Creation of the Universe

'In the beginning was the word.'
(W. Shakespeare)

ORIGINALLY there was nothing, obviously. And then, one day, there was a very big bang and the sky filled with heavenly bodies and rapidly became very much as it is today.

Big Bang Theory

This is known as the Big Bang Theory and, although nobody knows exactly what the Big Bang Theory is, I believe – along with many numerous other world famous historians – that, all in all, it offers a pretty cogent explanation of how the Universe began.

Opposite Direction

The Big Bang Theory (also known as the Theory of Relativity[1] or Quantum Theory) was, of course, discovered by Albert Einstein, the celebrated organist, missionary and director of *Battleship Potemkin*. He discovered that, although heavenly bodies generally look very still (unless they're a comet, of course, e.g. Hayley's Comet[2]), because of the Big Bang Theory, they, in fact, aren't. In fact, believe it or not, heavenly bodies are moving through the Universe at unbelievable speeds and often in the opposite direction.

1. Also discovered by Charles Dickens of course, in Australia.

2. Named after Hayley Mills, daughter of Sir John Mills, one of the greatest British actors in the whole world and star of *Pollyanna* and *The Parent Trap*.

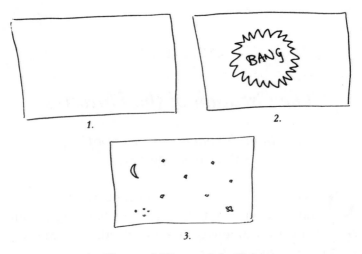

An Illustrated History of the Universe

A Bit of Luck

At the same time Heavenly bodies are *revolving incredibly fast as well*, although this is not the case for our own Sun, Moon and Earth fortunately. They are all stationary which is a bit of luck for us, otherwise living a normal life would be virtually impossible.

THINGS TO DO

1. Visit the world-famous Planetarium in London's delightful Marylebone Road. This is next door to Madame Tussauds. Then visit Madame Tussauds as well, seeing as you get in cheaper if you're already going to the Planetarium. If you are not from London, make sure you visit your local planetarium and waxworks, which are traditionally always in the same building.

2. Make a scale model of the Big Bang.

CHAPTER II

The Creation of the Earth

'This sceptred orb.'
(W. Shakespeare)

A ND so it was that a very big heavenly body appeared[1] in the as yet unformed sky and overlooked what is now the Earth, although it wasn't the Earth then, obviously.

And thus it stood, newly writ upon Heaven's mighty bosoms, until one day – suddenly and without warning – something remarkable occurred.

A Remarkable Occurrence

The flaming heavenly body that one day would be named the Sun by a species long since heretofore as yet undreamt of, of whom we ourselves are the inheritors, had a massive but unexpected nocturnal emission. Probably the first in the entire history of the World.

For why, we know not.

Upon what purpose, who could have foreseen?

But from deep within its fiery mantle there shot forth a little tiny gaseous new-born evaporable nomad. A deeply flatulent orb, volatized and aerifying, always on the brink of vanishing totally, yet containing, albeit unknown to itself, those seeds from whence all things would come that is or has been upon the Earth and will be upon the Earth also, in a manner of speaking.

1. Due to the Big Bang Theory. See Chapter I, page 3.

The Earth Created

And thus, without wishing to encumber the lay-reader with any more scientific data at this juncture, was the Earth created.[1]

THINGS TO DO

1. Paint a mural entitled 'The Creation of the Earth'.

2. Write an Essay entitled: 'How I would create the Earth if I was doing it.'

3. Create the Earth.

1. And then the Moon which shot out of the Earth in more or less the same way, a few years later. Probably, it is now believed, from Northampton.

CHAPTER III

The Volcanic Age

A Geological History of the Earth

'This burnished ball.'
(D. Dingle)

AFTER a few years, the Earth had numerous earth-quakes, volcanoes, continental rifts and mountains which went up and down all the time, until it looked more or less as it looks today, except for the seas which wasn't there, seeing as it hadn't rained yet.

For this reason, there were very few people at this juncture.

THINGS TO DO

1. Make a scale model of the Himalayas going up and down.

2. Begin your own collection of rock specimens. There are **three** basic kinds of rock. Sandstone, from which we get sand; chalk, from which we get chalk; limestone from which we get limes; and ignatious, named after Ignatious Loyola, the famous loyalist, which serves no purpose.

3. Swap them with your friends.

The Creation of the Midlands, 17,000,000,000,000,000,000 B.C.

CHAPTER IV

The Age of the Earth

*'Age cannot wither her nor staleness customize
her variable infinity.'*
(W. Shakespeare)

THERE are, of course, many theories of how old the
Earth is. Almost as many theories as there are grains
of sand in all the deserts there have ever been in the whole
world put together, I shouldn't wonder.

The ancient Hittites, for instance, believed we was
created on 9th February 252 B.C.

A Hittite

The Advent of Science

Such charmingly naive notions have now been disproved,
of course, by numerous modern world-famous historians
such as Lady Antonia Fraser and Simon Scharama and
by the advent of science, which the Hittites didn't have,
obviously, and has really only come in over the last few
years. Owing to miraculous scientific and electronic break-
throughs in such things as computer dating, it is now
possible to categorically prove that the Earth has been in
existence since at least 252,000 B.C. and probably began
on 22nd June.

The Dawn of Man

It has also been electronically proved that mankind – the men and women who are the subject of this work – did not start their historic journey until much more recently than has been supposed. In fact it is now thought that for many years there was no people on the Earth whatsoever. Just a load of birds, monkeys and plants. And before them, there wasn't even them! The Earth was simply a little revolting ball of dead mountains. Until it rained for approximately 15,000,000,000,000 years which it did for a number of rather complicated technical reasons, thus starting life [1] off as such.

THINGS TO DO

1. Make a scale model of the gaseous cloud of inorganic matter containing the seeds of life.

---

1. And weather.

CHAPTER V

Life Emerges

'Who knows from whence life did first emerge?'
(Anon)

AS is well known, the first life appeared in the seas which now covered the Earth, due to the rain. Except for the hills and mountains which was not covered, seeing as the rain stopped, on account of gravity.[1]

Early Amoeba (from which all life on earth developed)

Amoebas

The first life were amoebas, many of which were smaller than the human eye could see and thus similar to modern-day germs. Not surprisingly, they soon died out, owing to their size, and were immediately replaced by creatures who were bigger but spineless.

These included spineless lug-worms, spineless millipedes, spineless earwigs and spineless sea-slugs, which can't have made life beneath the ocean wave overly pleasant, seeing as they was all seventy or eighty foot long and slew each other with their massive tentacles willy-nilly whenever they felt like it.

1. Which was fortunate. It is a shocking thought that if it had never stopped raining, the earth would have simply become too heavy and sunk.

Spineless Sea-slug

Life Emerges

Fortunately, they all became small again, however, so that fish could evolve without fear of being strangled. And thus it was that life emerged from the sea.

Mankind

The Story of Mankind had truly begun, albeit as a Fish.

THINGS TO DO:

1. Make a scale-model of an amoeba.

CHAPTER VI

The Dawn of Man

'A man's a man for a' that.'
(Sophocles)

ALREADY we have noted the extraordinary and largely unknown fact that for many years there was no people on the Earth. But for how long?

When was it that Mankind finally appeared in the primogenital vista?

Daring Analogy

In order to answer these fascinating questions, let us begin with a simple but daring analogy. And compare the length of time that mankind has walked upon the Earth with the length of time that scientists, such as myself, now believe that the Earth has been here, on its own, without man on it, as it were.

Truly Amazing

Imagine, therefore, the Earth's history as being the entire length of the MI motorway, up to, and including, the Leeds underpass at Junction 47. If we was to do this, we would be truly amazed, as indeed I was, to discover that the history of humanity would have started *no sooner* than the roundabout at Hunslett,[1] which, of course, is a mere one and a half miles from the City Centre of Leeds itself, which is where, following the allusion through, we – the Human Race – stand today. At the centre of Leeds.

1. Raymond Box, my research assistant and trainee, has asked me to point out that his mother was born near Hunslett apparently.

Brent Cross

In other words – if the first spark of life leapt from the heart of the Sun and created the protoplasmic and bio-energetic cloudlet that became the Earth at Brent Cross,[1] then the ancestors of you and I (and Raymond) do not even begin the momentous journey that is, of course, the subject of this oeuvre until Junction 44.

Or even Junction 45!

And this remarkable and audacious analogy becomes even more unbelievable when we realize that the dinosaurs (popularly relegated to a mere thirty or forty years' worth of evolutionary trial and error) actually began to lumber through the petrified swamps of the prehistoric landscape at around Junction 21. And didn't finally peter out till the Moto Services at Trowell.[2] Twenty-seven miles later!

THINGS TO DO

1. Don't go driving all over the M1 just to test this theory. Take my word for it. The M1 is crowded enough as it is. Besides which, most of it has collapsed anyway clue to overcrowding in the inner cities and nationwide mining subsidence. Despite British Engineering, of course, which is famed throughout the world for such feats as the Clifton Suspension Bridge, the QE2 and the Taj Mahal.

The Taj Mahal

1. The historic shopping centre or 'mall' near the start of the M1 at the corner of Hendon Way and the North Circular. Historians now believe it was almost certainly named after my own company the National Theatre of Brent.

2. Near Nottingham. One of England's loveliest cities and home of T.E. Lawrence, the celebrated pornographic novelist.

CHAPTER VII

The Birth of the Dinosaurs

'Flee fro' the prees.'
(G. Chaucer)

THIS is even more astounding when we recollect that many dinosaurs had brains the size of Brussels sprouts. And those were the bright ones.

Baked Beans

Less fortunate dinosaurs had brains the size of baked beans and took at least six weeks of relentless brain-racking even to turn round. While some of the greatest dinosaurs that ever lived had brains the size of raisins and never *did* turn round. In other words, their brains were so small it took them most of their time just working out how to stay on four legs. Unless, of course, they had two legs, which took even longer.

Eating Difficulties

For the dinosaur, eating, for instance, became a massively complex process and a simple two- or three-course dinner could take months from start to finish. The main difficulty with eating for the dinosaur was that his brain – being so pathetically minuscule – had no room in it for what we in the medical profession call 'Memory Retention'. In other words, not only did the dinosaur have extreme difficulty in remembering what was food and what wasn't, but also, and more crucial, he was always forgetting what feeling hungry felt like. So that many dinosaurs never actually knew they were hungry and often dropped dead without ever having had a meal.

A Problem Solved

This – I hope – will once and for all solve the so-called mystery of why the dinosaurs died out. In a nutshell – the dinosaurs died out because they were stupid.

★ ★ ★

HOW WE KNOW NO. I

The dinosaurs that did eat tended generally to be either carnivorous or herbaceous, and we can tell by their skulls which one they were by examining its teeth. (*See illustration.*)

Fig. 1.
Carnivorous Dinosaur

Fig. 2.
Herbaceous Dinosaur.

(*Note: The carnivorous teeth are pointed and the herbaceous flat so as to chew numerous plants with.*)

It goes without saying, obviously, that the carnivorous dinosaurs, being meat-eaters, tended to eat the herbaceous dinosaur, seeing as the herbaceous dinosaur (a) couldn't bite the carnivore back because of his flat teeth, (b) couldn't turn round anyway (see p. 14) and (c) didn't actually want to bite the carnivore because he was a vegetarian with a vegetarian instinct which is basically to find meat repulsive.[1] We can imagine, therefore, the anguish of one such herbaceous dinosaur, his little tail already caught

---

1. I happen to know this, because I myself am a very strict vegetarian. Apart from tuna, fish and chicken.

in the vice-like jaws of a Tyrannosaurus and his minuscule brain working overtime, sending contradictory messages up and down his tragically massive body. 'Bite, Bite!' says one. 'You must protect your life.' 'No, No!' says the other. 'Do not bite him. You do not eat meat. You are a vegetarian. Besides which he is a creature of the earth like you. He is your brother. You love all creatures.'

This raging inner dialogue probably taxed the dinosaur to such an extent that it died of a heart attack anyway, though presumably that would have been a better option than being savaged to death by a frenzied Velociraptor who's just discovered he's hungry after ninety-five years.

Two famous dinosaurs. The long-necked Diplodocus (diplo = long; docus = neck) *talks to a Triceratops, the celebrated three-horned dinosaur* (tricera = horns; tops = on the top of his head).

THINGS TO DO

1. See the two archaeological films: *One Million Years B.C.* and *When Dinosaurs Ruled The Earth*, starring Raquel Welch. Also more recently the popular film *Dinosaur* about a dinosaur and a load of monkeys starring Dame Joan Plowright as a Brontosaurus in some of the most remarkable make-up in cinema history.

CHAPTER VIII

The Advent of Mammals

'Life is a mixture of sunshine and rain,
Good things and bad things, pleasure and pain,
We can't all have sunshine, but it's certainly true
There is never a cloud the sun doesn't shine through.'
(Helen Steiner Rice — *Just for You*)

A FEW years later something remarkable occurred. All the Dinosaurs died out and loads of mammals appeared. They immediately lasted millions of years longer than the dinosaurs owing to a number of biological advantages the dinosaurs never had.

Rudimentary mammal

Advantages

The five chief advantages of being a mammal as opposed to a dinosaur are:

1.   Mammals are furrier.[1]

---

1. Except for man who is generally devoid of hair (see page 26). And elephants obviously. And rhinos. And hippos. And whales. And hedgehogs. I was actually fully aware of them, thank you Raymond.

2. Mammals are smaller.[1]
3. Mammals are born alive.
4. Dinosaurs are reptiles.

Man

It should be noted that mammals came after dinosaurs but before man, although few people realize that man is also a mammal seeing as he is born alive and has breasts.

Rudimentary man (note similarity to rudimentary mammal)

THINGS TO DO

Make a list of the advantages of **(a)** being an insect as opposed to a fish, **(b)** being born alive, **(c)** living in a bungalow.

---

1. And therefore able to hide easily. For a fifth-century Diplodocus, the length of twelve London buses end to end, finding a suitable hiding place would have been well-nigh impossible. Even if it had a brain the size of a bungalow. Mind you, if it had had a brain the size of a bungalow, its neck would have collapsed and it couldn't have moved anywhere anyway. It would have been a phenomenally intelligent vegetable.

CHAPTER IX

The Dawn of Man

'A man's a man for a' that.'
(Lulu)

AND thus it was the stage was set for the Dawn of Man himself.

Man

However it is essential to realize that man didn't just appear from nowhere. It wasn't all animals and plants one day and then animals and plants and man the next. In other words, he didn't just wander out from behind a petrified forest looking like any common or garden man in the street.

Lemur

No. Man *became* man. In other words, like everything else, he was not a man originally. Originally, he was a ring-tailed lemur. Well, actually, he was a fish. Or rather two fish. Which means that before he was a fish he was an amoeba. Which means of course, that before that he wasn't anything. In other words, and to cut a long story short, we have all evolved from absolutely nothing, which is a pretty remarkable thought when you think about it.

Scantily Clad

Thus was born the famous Theory of Evolution (or Gravity) which was of course discovered by Charles Darwin, the celebrated Australian novelist who also discovered Relativity, jet propulsion and New Zealand and whose name is remembered throughout Australia in such places as Darwin, Port Darwin, Little Darwin, Greater Darwin, Darwin-on-Tees and Wagga Wagga. He soon moved to the Galapagos Islands in the South Pacific where he became enamoured of a scantily-clad native girl after which they had the Mutiny on the Bounty and she bore him many offspring including Ned Kelly, Baz Luhrmann, Alice Springs and Thomas Cooke the well-known travel agent who also discovered Australia and New Zealand.[1]

The Discovery of Australia and New Zealand by Thomas Cooke

1. At this point I would just like to take this opportunity of introducing myself and my research assistant Raymond to any new Australian friends we might be making as a result of their possibly reading this volume. I would like to say – on behalf of both of us – that I have, in fact, had the enormous privilege of meeting a number of Australian people in my life, all of whom I have found extremely courteous and interesting in nearly every aspect. I have also met a number of New Zealand people as well and they have all been very nice too. Anyway many of them have told me they feel deprived of all the culture and history of the British Isles of which they was once part. As a result I believe that a cultural lecture tour of Australia and New Zealand (and then possibly Fiji and Tahiti and Tonga and all them tropical islands where ladies give you flowers at the airport) might help 'bridge the gap' between our nations and if an offer did happen to be forthcoming in this regard I can absolutely guarantee that we would not only be honoured but also available; or if not Raymond, who has his foam shop in Staines to attend to, I most certainly would, for a reasonable fee obviously, at a couple of days' notice. Please contact Nick Herm Books or, if they're closed, me personally.

POPULAR MISCONCEPTIONS NO. I

Life emerged from the sea. This is true. But it is certainly *not* true that animals, birds and plants etc. just trooped out on to the beach in the perfectly formed state in which we know them today. All these creatures, in fact, evolved from two prehistoric fish who are now extinct but who took the decision on behalf of all living things that would ever be (apart from modern-day fish obviously) that the land had more going for it than the sea.

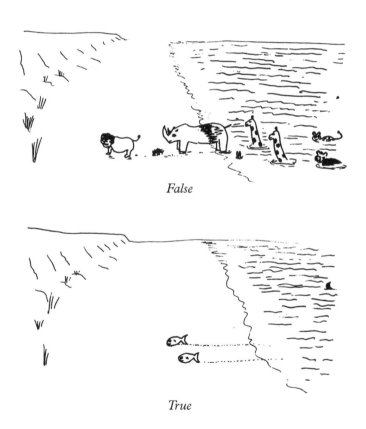

False

True

But what a foolhardy idea it must have seemed at the time. To turn your back on a pleasant warm ocean bed, with little coral reefs and rocky coves and an endless supply of trilobites and plankton and heave your great floundering legless body on to the sand, beneath a burning sun, and then start trudging off on fins into a landscape that, let's be frank, wasn't exactly the Tivoli Gardens.

What on earth possessed them?

We may never know.

THINGS TO DO

1. Write short notes on the following:

Jet propulsion.

Wagga Wagga.

New Zealand.

Dame Kiri Te Kanawa.

2. Write an essay entitled 'Australia and New Zealand – why I would like to visit it.'

CHAPTER X

Man after he was a Lemur

'*So what come of man*
After he was a lemur?'
(Milton)

LET us now return to the evolutionary journey of man after he was a lemur. Naturally he didn't become a man straight after being a lemur. In order to facilitate becoming a man he became a Primate first. After which he become a man. Or 'homo erectus' as they became known. Which is what we are today, obviously. Unless we're a woman, of course. Which many of us are as well. Fortunately for the Human Race, if I may say so! Naturally, however, those early humans would have been a very far cry from you or me in terms of looks. Hardly Michelangelo's David,[1] in other words.

Michelangelo's David (artist's reconstruction)

1. The famous statue by Leonardo da Vinci.

Dinosaur copra.

LITTLE-KNOWN FACTS NO. I

This is the fossil of a dinosaur dropping. It is the size of Wembley Stadium and is called a coprolite (from copra = a large amount of unpleasant non-essential matter and lite = that which is dropped from a great height). The study of coprolites is called coprology and is carried out by coprologists who often devote their entire lives to the study of these great and terrible artefacts.

Coprologists have few friends and generally live alone.

★ ★ ★

Mouth-Watering

Not, of course, that we can all claim to look like Michelangelo's David. Some of us, obviously, but not everybody. I, for instance, have been blessed with rather above average looks, I'm happy to say (see front cover) – a feature noted by a number of people, particularly certain members of the fairer sex as it happens. But even those less physically appealing than myself (like Raymond for instance) would have looked positively mouth-watering in comparison with those early hominids, lumbering through the primordial rain forests with great hairy bodies, pointed foreheads, massive jaws and horribly prehensile thumbs. In other words, although they was in fact humans, they still looked identical to the apes which they had just been before they became human. They was in fact humans trapped in an ape's body. Which must have been an extraordinarily painful experience if you think about it.

So – I hear you ask – if he was, to all intents and purposes, an ape, how come he become a human like we are today?

For one simple, essential and obvious reason.

HE HAD A HUMAN BRAIN.

Where he found it need not concern us. For nobody knows. Suffice it to say he had one. In other words, he was only a great hairy primate on the outside. Inside he was as human as you or I.

Carol Vordeman

Needless to say, we didn't all turn overnight into Carol Vordeman, probably one of the most intelligent people in the world and one of the most charming too, if I may say so. Not that I have had the pleasure of meeting her personally, but judging by her very warm television manner that has endeared her to millions across the globe. In other words, brains weren't always what they are nowadays. And the early human brain – while being massively more advanced than ape, dinosaur or amoeba brains – was certainly not the intricate piece of equipment we walk around with nowadays.

The Development of the Brain

The *earliest* human brain was approximately the equivalent size and, in some respects, texture of a King Edward potato. Its main advantage over previous brains being that while dinosaurs' and apes' brains gave them rudimentary skills such as walking, eating and going to the toilet, they didn't give them the essential brainal requisites of knowing *when* or *where* to do these things.

TEACHERS: PLEASE NOTE THE NEXT PAGE CARRIES SOME EXPLICIT BIOLOGICAL DETAIL AND MAY NOT BE APPROPRIATE FOR YOUNGER CHILDREN.

Going to the Toilet

Take going to the toilet, for example. The Dinosaur's raisin-sized brain, for instance, would just go to the toilet anywhere, regardless of time and place, which must have been unpleasant – seeing as dinosaurs' bladders were often the size of three cricket pitches end to end, and, worse, their 'bowel disposal equipment', as it is known geologically, would often pass non-essential foodmatter or copras (see 'Little Known Facts No 1', p. 24) equivalent to the size of seven First World War Zeppelins.

Anyway, brains expanded and developed more and more features until the modern-day brain appeared which controls not only the complete human orgasm but is also capable of a staggering number of capabilities, many of which we don't know we have, like bending forks, turning tennis balls inside out, flying in our astral bodies and E.S.N. In fact, the modern-day brain is now so well developed that if it got any bigger it would burst through our heads and we would probably die of brain exposure.

Revolutionary Idea

And so it was the advent of the human brain that gave man the revolutionary idea of standing on two legs, thus setting him apart, once and for all, from every other living creature on the planet, all of whom have four feet. (Except for kangaroos and fish.)[1]

Hair Loss

Another thing that had to occur before man became man and stopped being a Primate was that all the fur and hair had to drop off his body which it rapidly started doing almost immediately, thank goodness, and is a bit of luck for humans living nowadays.

---

1. And millipedes, centipedes, flies, bluebottles, birds, octopuses, spiders, jellyfish, seagulls, prawns and snakes. Thank you, Raymond.

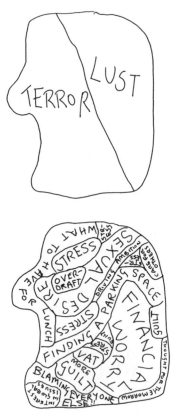

Comparison of the brains of Prehistoric and Modern Man

THINGS TO DO

1. Make a scale model of a lemur turning into an ape.

2. Dissect a brain.

3. Write an essay entitled: 'Copras – discuss.'

CHAPTER XI

The Emergence of Civilization

'Civilization gradually emerged.'
(D. Dingle)

AND so – at last – Civilization emerged. And not before time to be honest! As rudimentary men and women – with their ever-complicating brains and rapidly moulting bodies – began to venture across the shifting continents of the Earth on their endless quest for those things that we, now, of course, take so much for granted – water, berries, sheep, paint, God, mammoths, to name but a few.

Mammoth

Alarming

I say 'shifting', not as a passing comment on man's fickle territorial habits and ever-changing alliances (which well I might if I was commenting on the alarming behavioural patterns of modern humankind), but because the planetary land masses was still banging and shifting about and changing places and generally re-aligning themselves all over the place. Still deciding, as it were, on how finally to form themselves when they finally stopped shifting. In other words – even as those first heroic rudimentary men and women were taking their first tentative steps upon

28

terra firma – Africa was still joined to North America, Australia was part of Holland, China was bashing against Scotland, and Norway was still an indiscriminate lump on the edge of Peru. In other words, *terra firma* was not very firm at all, basically.

Benefits

However, there were benefits. For many years, for instance, and not many people know this, *there was no English Channel* joining Great Britain to the Continent. So that a day trip to France, for instance, would simply have been a question of walking. Which must have come as a welcome relief on a journey otherwise fraught with volcanoes, woolly rhinos, cave painting smugglers and disused mammoth traps. Unfortunately, however, because of the planetary shifting, no land mass could ever be relied upon to stay in the same place for any guaranteed length of time. Thus one of the greatest terrors of the epoch was what scientists now call *Land Disappearance*. Many was the time, in other words, that a troupe of British cavemen would reappear after a week-end in France or Belgium, with their baguettes and bucket of hot coals, only to find that Britain had totally disappeared and was in fact at that moment nuzzling up to Tasmania, nine thousand miles away.

Heart-Rending

Land Replacement, on the other hand, was an even more heart-rending problem. When you'd wake up in the morning and find yourself floating past Tibet. These were difficult and rudimentary times.[1] The only thing there was no shortage of at this time was, in fact, stones, which were everywhere. Hence the name of this age became known as the Stone Age – as it is to this day. Although Civilization was definitely emerging at this time – as stated earlier – it

1. To put it mildly.

couldn't *totally* emerge until the Stone Age, which was very uncivilized obviously, had actually finished. Which it did quite soon, fortunately, seeing as it only lasted ten or eleven years.

The correct technical or archaeological term for Stone-Age people was *cavemen*, seeing as they lived in caves. Which are generally found in rural areas such as the Peak District.[1] Cavemen and Cavewomen decorated their caves with cave paintings although, unfortunately, they were appallingly unlifelike and crude.

Stone Age family and pet

THINGS TO DO

1. Construct a Stone-Age lunar observatory.

2. Visit a Stone-Age ruin.

3. Discuss Civilization generally.

---

1. Note to overseas readers: the Peak District is an attractive beauty-spot in England's Derbyshire. It is probably best described as a slightly more compact version of the Rockies or the Barrier Reef. If you ever fancy a week-end away in the Peak District or any of our lovely beauty-spots, please don't hesitate to get in touch with the English Tourist Board or, directly, with Nick Herm Books Ltd., where Mr Herm himself will be only too happy to advise on accommodation, suggested clothing, bargain fares etc.

CHAPTER XII

The Iron Age

'This, truly, is an iron age!'
(Anon)

AFTER the Stone Age was the Iron Age, which also came just before the gradual emergence of Civilization and was very interesting.

The Iron Age was famous for Stonehenge, which came from Wales by boat.

Famous Iron-Age queens was Boadicea, and everything was made of iron generally.

THINGS TO DO

1. Find out more about the Iron Age.

Queen Boadicea (Iron Age ancestor of our own Queen)

CHAPTER XIII

The Bronze Age

'All that glistens is not bronze.'
(W. Shakespeare)

THE Bronze Age also came a few years later and was also very interesting.

THINGS TO DO

1. Make a Bronze-Age hat.

CHAPTER XIV

The Egyptians

'Pharoah's a jolly good fellow.'
(Popular Egyptian song)

IT was then that Civilization emerged with a number of very famous ancient Civilizations. One of the most famous ancient Civilizations was the Egyptians, whom I find personally a very interesting people, not least because of their interest in reincarnation, which I have personally experienced (*see page 35*).

The Sphinx (now extinct)

Besides building the pyramids (*see page 40*) and doing the Sphinx (*see above*), the Egyptians became renowned for their wall-paintings, which aren't overly lifelike, to put it mildly. In fact they had no idea of perspective whatsoever, but then again nobody did at that time.

Bondage

The Egyptians were an exotic people, who wore small kilts, were generally bald and spent much of their time feasting, dancing, hunting hippo and keeping their slaves in bondage. They was also famous for embalming their ancestors, cats, livestock and other people. Naturally it was the Pharaohs (similar to our Queen) and the priests

(The Archbishop of Canterbury) who done the hippo hunting and the embalming. The working-class people and the enslaved nations lived in windowless holes in the ground and spent their entire lives making twenty-ton bricks for the pyramids (*see page 40*). They had no leisure time which meant it was impossible to have any hobbies such as rock-climbing or bird-watching. In fact the closest they got to any wild life was the Pharaoh's crocodiles, to whom they were fed periodically, either as a warning, as a mystic ceremony, or just anyway.

An Egyptian

Mummy

When the Pharaoh died, he was, of course, embalmed himself, along with three or four hundred hand-picked slaves, who was embalmed with him. He was then called a Mummy. Being a hand-picked embalmed slave was obviously a much sought-after position and definitely preferable to making bricks in a four-foot windowless hole in the Nile Delta. For this reason, slaves had their names on the Local Embalmment List from an early age. At the time of a Pharaoh's death, Cairo was always packed with young hopefuls hoping to be spotted in the souks and smoky bars and plucked from brick-making obscurity into a life of eternal embalmment. Interest in

Embalming a mummy

embalmment fell off dramatically in the sixth century, however, when it was discovered that embalmment entailed being killed first.

Reincarnation

The Egyptians believed in reincarnation, which is a theory, popular today, that we have all lived before in another time and endlessly live again, going round and round and being different people and animals and so forth till we become totally enlightened and have no need to live on the earth no more.

Yul Brynner

I have researched this subject quite considerably with numerous experts under hypnotic regression, and I can now reveal that I myself was Rameses II, the scourge of the Hebrews, for which I am, of course, very sorry, and would like to make it quite clear that I will never do anything like that again, and was played by Yul Brynner in the renowned film, *The Ten Commandments*, which is one of the greatest films ever made. I also have evidence I was Alfred the Great, Gandhi, Robin Hood, Abraham Lincoln, Joan of Arc and Freud. Some of this evidence has come about through hypnosis and some through inexplicable bodily sensations. For instance, I now have incontrovertible evidence that I am the reincarnated spirit of Pablo Picasso, the world famous modern painter who died in 1973, as I have recently begun to feel strange psychic tremors in Spanish restaurants and a driving inner compulsion to paint cubes. I have also undergone experiments in which I have had tantalizing glimpses of past lives *which I haven't yet had.* These include a Hollywood teen idol, two world leaders, a Pope, a fabulously wealthy heart specialist and a member of the Royal Family (probably King).[1]

Robin Hood

A Final Note

One of the great tragedies in the film world is that Omar Sharif – one of the greatest actors in the world, and star of *Lawrence of Arabia, Ghengis Khan, The Bridge over the River Kwai,* etc – has never acted in a film about ancient Egypt. This is particularly sad seeing as Mr Sharif is actually Egyptian and therefore would be ideal casting. May I suggest that the next time an ancient Egyptian film comes up he should be immediately signed up before he loses interest.

1. In similar experiments that I have conducted with Raymond, we discovered that his past lives included an eighteenth-century chamber-maid, a 1930s library attendant and an unknown passer-by. All intriguing in their way, obviously, though not quite as spectacular as mine, it goes without saying.

And thus it was that the sun set on the mighty Egyptian Empire.

THINGS TO DO

1. Draw the inside of a slave's hovel.

2. Embalm a dead creature.

3. Design a tomb for a friend.

★ ★ ★

POPULAR MISCONCEPTIONS NO. 2

The Pyramids

These were first discovered by Lord Carter of Caernarvon, the famous Welsh archaeologist. Resulting, of course, in the immediate death of himself and his heirs, owing to the celebrated curse left there by the Pharaohs for such an eventuality and from which his family are still perishing to this day.

I, along with many other famous archaeologists, have marvelled at these mysterious edifi, standing like silent sentinels, witnesses to the cruel passing of time. I, too, have paced the sands wondering what purpose these buildings served and to what strange use they were put by that people about whom we know all too little. Finally I reached the conclusion that each pyramid was in fact the *roof* of some form of regal dwelling-house. A country retreat, perhaps, or an ancient Chequers, where the Pharaoh and his cabinet could quietly order their governmental tasks, far from the noisesome hurly-burly of downtown Cairo. A regal dwelling that had sunk inch by inch over the centuries into the shifting desert sands, leaving only the massive stone-built roof remaining to public gaze.

However, I should now like to make known an extra-ordinary discovery that has recently come to my attention. Namely that *there is, in fact, nothing below these imposing monuments*. They are simply standing on top of the sand. And were probably used, according to certain evidence that has just come into my possession, as *tombs*. To put the Pharaohs in. Once they'd been embalmed, obviously.

To be perfectly honest, I always felt the old 'Roof Theory' to be rather dubious, owing to the fact that the sloping roof was invented for the rainy climate. If the pyramids *were* roofs, then the fact that they are at least 2,000 feet tall would be massively disproportionate to the fact that rain is a totally unknown quantity in Egypt. Also there are no chimneys, which there would be if it was a roof, obviously.

And thus it was that the sun set on the mighty Egyptian empire.

★ ★ ★

THE STORY OF MOSES
A famous story

One of the most famous stories about the Egyptians was the story of Moses, who was put by his mother in the Nile in a Hebrew linen basket daubed in river mud so that it would not sink. Pharaoh's daughter happened to be bathing in the Nile on that day and she saw the Hebrew linen basket and did not think nothing more of it seeing as people had no concern about river pollution in those days generally and chucked all and sundry in there without a thought. But then it was she heard a baby's cry and quickly bade her serving maid to rescue the basket, which she done.

Pharaoh's daughter had never had any children because she never had the interest but, as soon as she saw the tiny babe and his little manly fists, did yearn for him mightily. And thus said unto her handmaids:

'He will be mine own baby but I must have a nurse-maid to look after him as my days are taken up doing my make-up and bathing in asses' milk.'

Whereupon immediately Moses's sister Miriam leapt forth from the reeds and said:

'Oddly enough I am a professional nursemaid, oh Mighty Pharaoh's daughter. I could not help overhearing what you were saying.'

'Very well, Hebrew slave, you will be his nursemaid, but what will I call him?'

'Excuse me, oh Mighty Daughter of the incarnated Sun on Earth, you could call him Moses.'

'Moses?'

'Possibly.'

'But does that not mean: "He who will lead and deliver his people out of bondage, will see God in a burning bush, get the Ten Commandments, be responsible for endless frogs and locusts and boils and the deaths of all the Egyptian first-born, drown the Egyptian armies and Pharaoh personally in the Red Sea and set free all the Hebrews so that the Egyptians will have to build the pyramids themselves"?'

'No, it means: "He who was washed up in a laundry basket and found by Pharaoh's daughter".'

'How lovely. In that case I will call him Moses.'

Pharoah's Daughter

Thus the story goes on. A very beautiful story known throughout the world and filmed – as I have already mentioned – as *The Ten Commandments* starring Charlton

Heston, Yul Brynner and Omar Sharif. Unfortunately, we do not have time in this work to go into the whole of the story of Moses, owing to the fact that it is extremely long.

And thus it was that the Sun set on the mighty Egyptian Empire.

The Pyramids

CHAPTER XV

The Chinese Empire

ᘐᘝᘱᘦᘒᘝ ᘲᘲᘬᘱᘒ

(Confucius)

THE Chinese Empire is one of the oldest Empires in the world and existed until recently without anyone knowing about it. Apart from the Chinese, obviously.

The Chinese People

The Chinese People were generally very down-trodden and ill. They made their living as slaves to the Emperors, for which they were not paid, owing to the fact that they were peasants. They had no say whatsoever in their own government and if anyone *did* say anything they were immediately killed without redress. Hence their reputation, to this day, as a rather unforthcoming people. They generally caught horrible diseases and had no form of heating, lighting, medical treatment or hope.

The Emperors

The Emperors, on the other hand, lived very pleasant lives in large paper-built pagodas and spent most of their time cultivating silkworms, eating lychees and worshipping their ancestors. This was known as Ancestor Worship and is based on the belief that as soon as an ancestor dies he becomes a god. This was a very clever circumlocution around the problem, redolent in many societies, that some ancestors want to be gods before they're dead. The point is you can't *be* an ancestor if you're still alive, obviously. So it was impossible for the ancestors of the Chinese Emperors to become gods until they was completely deceased. Which saved considerable internecine difficulties, not surprisingly.

Dynasties

The Emperors themselves ruled what was known as Dynasties, which, generally speaking, lasted about five hundred years before moving on to the next one. The Emperor would rule the Dynasty and the Dynasty would rule the Peasants.

Chinese Political and Economic Infrastructure (detailed diagram)

Each Dynasty obviously had its own laws, fashions and behavioural modes and most important of all had its own Vase, which as soon as a new Dynasty came in was immediately sent out and copied throughout the land. So, for instance, when the Ming Dynasty came in, everyone had to make Ming vases and send back their previous vases which happened to be Ch'ung vases. These were then smashed up by the government in ancient vase disposal units, similar to our modern-day bottle banks. Some people didn't return their vases but buried them or sent back fakes

Ming Vase   *Other Chinese Vases*

and then nipped over the border to sell them as antiques in Japan or Hong Kong. Vase smuggling was punishable by death, but then that wasn't particularly unusual, seeing as virtually everything was punishable by death.

The Shang Dynasty

The first Dynasty was the Shang Dynasty, who ruled from the earliest times and was already drinking out of tea-cups, while Stone-Age man in Britain was grubbing for wood-lice and eating each other's brains.[1] The Shang Dynasty became obsessed with Chinese cooking and, although they also invented the wok and prawn balls, they lost the hearts of the man in the street and their days was numbered.

A heartless Anatoloian horse salesman

The Chou Dynasty

The Shang Dynasty was displaced by the Chou Dynasty, a cruel and heartless race of Anatolian horse salesmen, who swept down from the south and cleaned up within two or three months. They had little interest in cooking,

1. This unpleasant Stone-Age habit was not mentioned in previous chapters owing to the fact that I've only just heard about it on an intellectual television quiz show that I happen to enjoy watching. Apparently they ate each other's brains to make themselves cleverer. Which is certainly not something you'd catch me doing, even if I was offered a bowlful of Simon Shchrarma's brains.

although they did introduce Chinese cabbage, and thus revolutionized the making of coleslaw.

Cabbage

Marco Polo, or Mark Long as he was called in England, discovered Chinese cabbage and introduced it into Europe, particularly France, who was so impressed they decided to use the name of the Great Chinese Dynasty as their word for cabbage.

The Chinese

The Chinese invented most things, as they do to this day. They invented the Peking Opera, the most famous of which was *The Mikado* by Gilbert O' Sullivan, and also books, written from back to front and from bottom to top for no reason that has yet been discerned.

They also invented banshee wailers, tin-openers, hydroelectricity, Aladdin heaters, kimonos, the take-away meal and acupuncture.[1]

Cultural Revolution

The Chinese people's lot became more and more unbearable under the Dynasties, so they had a Cultural Revolution which meant everyone wore the same suit and made farm machinery, but was much more cultured as a result.

Chinese rice salesman

1. The impaling of the body on numerous razor-sharp needles for long periods of time in small rooms in North London.

44

THINGS TO DO

1. Write a diagrammatic analysis of Confucian thought.

2. Make a Chinese hat or useful lampshade (see diagram below).

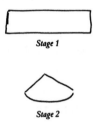

Stage 1

Stage 2

CHAPTER XVI

The Glory that was Crete

Q: *A Cretan housewife went to pay her taxes. She had five pounds in one ear and a pound note in the other. What was she?*
A: *Six pounds in arrears.*
(Famous Cretan Joke)

Cradle of Western Civilization

AFTER the Chinese Empire, the next major empire was Crete who were the cradle of Western Civilization and lived on the attractive holiday isle of Crete, famed for its olive groves, windmills and old-world Venetian ports throbbing with music, art and romantic night-life.

Conclusion

Unfortunately they didn't last long and suddenly died out after a few years.

THINGS TO DO

1. Paint a picture of Crete dying out.

2. Why not visit Cretan Magic Travel Shop, 109 Regent Street, London W1? Present a copy of this book and claim a 50 per cent discount on any holiday of your choice.

I. THE AUTHOR

*with the entire company of the National Theatre of Brent
(Raymond Box) engaged in historical research.*

2a. 10 Downing Street, seat of the Prime Minister of Great Britain.

*2b. Eros. Probably the most loved historic monument in the world.
Visited by tens of thousands of people per day.*

2c. Big Ben (built by Benjamin Disraeli).

*2d. Trafalgar Square (the world-famous landmark, built by
the Arts Council to commemorate the Battle of Trafalgar Square).*

3. MISS JULIET STEVENSON

*Probably one of this country's greatest living prima donnas,
in my opinion.*

4. MICHELANGELO'S BIRTHPLACE

No 96, Pinham Drive, Bournemouth
(see Little Known Facts, No. 3).

5. FOUR FAMOUS BRITISH KINGS

(enacted by Raymond Box)

5a. Richard the Lionheart
5b. Richard III

5c. Henry VIII
5d. Good King Wenceslas

6a. Buckingham Palace (seen from side).

6b. Victoria Station (notice also the Shakespeare pub, an original Elizabethan tavern where Shakespeare is believed to have written his best-known works).

7. FOUR HISTORICAL LEGENDS

(enacted by the author)

7a. Lawrence of Arabia

7b. Ben Hur

7c. Lorenzo the Magnificent

7d. Sir Francis Drake

8. TWO INFAMOUS HISTORICAL CHARACTERS

Lucrezia and Victor Borgia – renowned for their stormy and incestuous love affairs all over Venice.

CHAPTER XVII

The Greeks

'It's all Greek to me.'
(Timon of Athens)

The Greeks

THE Greeks came straight after Crete and swept immediately into Greece for obvious reasons, thus becoming the Greek Empire as they are to this day. They are probably the most famous of all the major Civilizations we've had so far although many historians will dispute this, particularly Egyptologists who will doubtless say that Egypt is all, seeing as they invented the pyramids and Cleopatra's needle etc.

The Egyptians

But to this argument I would say simply this: Fair enough! The Egyptians *did* invent the pyramids and so forth. Nobody disputes this. They also built Abu Simbel and the pharaohs. *But are they in use today?* This is the question. How often do you see a two-thousand-foot-high pyramid in an English graveyard? How often do we use a sphinx or Abu Simbel in our common-or-garden daily life? The answer is brief but short. Never. Or at least very rarely.

The Greeks

The Greeks, on the other hand, invented endless essential and labour-saving things that are in use to this day. Crockery, the Olympic Games, the Coliseum, olives, words, tyranny, the Oedipus complex, hang-gliding. The list is endless. To my mind there is no question about it. Without the Egyptians we would simply be short of a couple of mummies and the Suez Canal. Whereas, without the Greeks, we would almost certainly not be able to stand where we stand today, in a manner of speaking.

The Suez Canal

A Remarkable New Theory

The Greeks are obviously most famous for what they done in Greece, which they ruled (and very well, too, if I may say so), but it is my belief that they also ruled many other parts of the world as well, in particular the United States of America. This is a remarkable new theory which happens to be my own, as it happens, and I would like to take this opportunity, at this point, of pausing briefly to examine it in considerable detail at this juncture.

Did the Greeks Reach America?

A quick glance at the map of the United States reveals three Corinths, thirteen Athenses, nine Spartas, five Venices and one Thermopylae. Now, I have never been one for jumping to outlandish conclusions but surely this must be more than pure coincidence. As we have already seen, the Greeks invented nearly everything the world has ever known. So wouldn't one trip across the Atlantic have been a piece of cake to such a people?

Besides, who else but a race of deep intellectuals would have thought to call a couple of wooden shacks

58

and an outside toilet *Thermopylae?* Or *Keffalonia?* Which are feats of spelling in themselves. Some dice-wielding Billy the Kid, reeking of alcohol, cheroots and saddle soap? He'd have called it 'Shenandoah' or 'Moosejaw' or something equally non-classical. The point I'm making is that the very *names* of Ancient Greece are extremely poetic, cultural and intellectual words in their own right and were clearly invented by highly cultured Greek philosophers and experts and not by some psychopathic gun-toting cowpoke who just happened – coincidentally – to dream it up for some derelict silver-mine in Nebraska.

Conclusion

To sum up, it is a well-known fact that the Greeks was the first people to conquer the world under Alexander Nevsky, the well-known king. I'm not saying he reached everywhere, obviously. But he definitely reached a lot of places. *So why not the United States of America?*

Decline

Tragically it wasn't long before the Greeks started declining which was due to excessive theatre-going and lolling about in the nude all day. In fact Greek nudity had reached epidemic proportions.

But how did it actually begin?

Greek Nudity

Greek nudity began, innocently enough, in sporting activities which you had to do in the nude for religious reasons. This was mainly seeing as the Greek gods (Zeus, Jove, Mars, Bounty, etc.) was all completely nude. As can be seen in numerous famous Greek paintings such as 'Botticelli's Venus', 'Clash of the Titans', 'Zorba The Greek' etc. In other words, if you was a Greek athlete, you weren't even allowed so much as a pair of Greek plimsolls. Whatever the sport, chucking the discus, doing the hurdles, tennis, you had to be totally bare. Which was fine, obviously, if you had a very aesthetically beautiful body like Torvill and Dean or someone. Or me, to be honest. But a little cruel if you didn't, clearly. Like various people I know, for instance, who – without naming names obviously – have very unappealing bodies, to put it mildly.

The Decline of Greek Nudity

Anyway, most Greeks had a very attractive body, fortunately, so it wasn't long before everyone was walking round stark naked, showing it off everywhere and putting it on vases which was, of course, the thin end of the wedge and which led, as we have seen, to the entire collapse of Greece, within a few days.

A Famous Greek Thinker

The only Grecian, in fact, who didn't have an aesthetically beautiful body, was Socrates, the famous Greek thinker, who, from the photos, was extremely overweight with a receding forehead and a bit of manky hair on the back of his head. For this reason, he put hemlock in his retsina and died in the bath of his Athenian hotel. He was discovered the next morning by the chamber-maid, surrounded by his dietary supplements, his exercise bicycle and his Grecian 2000.

The Olympic Games

The Greeks of course invented the Olympic Games which was held on the top of Mount Olympus, apart from the Winter Olympics which were held in Switzerland or Aspen, Colorado, due to the snow. The Olympic Games was invented, as is well known, to unite all nations upon the Earth, but were a smaller affair than what they are now seeing as everyone else was either still very prehistoric (United Kingdom, France, Belgium etc.), didn't yet exist

(Africa, Russia, India, Australia, South America etc.) or were only interested in board games (China). For this reason the Greeks constantly won all the medals, which rather defeated the object and, as a result, became tragically spineless, as any psychiatrist will tell you.

The End Of Greece

And thus it was that the sun set on the mighty Greek Empire. And a great relief to all concerned, probably.

THINGS TO DO

1. Build a scale model of Sophocles.

2. Write an imaginary diary of a tragically spineless Greek athlete.

3. Design an ancient Greek.

4. Write a play about the Oedipus complex in the style of Greek tragedy.

The end of the Greeks

CHAPTER XVIII

The Grandeur that was Rome

'Nihil est impossible, sed certain homines sunt.'
(Old Roman witticism)

The Birth of Rome

THE Romans were the next Civilization after the Greeks and were generally similar, wearing similar types of helmets and buildings and generally doing similar kinds of things. Fortunately, however, the Romans were more sensible and generally older than the Greeks which can be seen immediately by their dress (*see below*).

So How Was it the Birth of Rome Come About?

As is well known, the birth of Rome happened in a staggeringly short space of time. One moment there was a load of decadent nude Greeks flopping about all over the place, going to all-night parties and so forth, then suddenly there was the Romans. Coming out of nowhere, covered in shields, hurtling about *Italia* (Italy) or *Gaul* (France) or *Hispaniola* (Scotland) in wedge-shaped formations, taking everything over everywhere, and stabbing their adversaries in the legs with their little short stabbing swords. The reason behind this meteoric rise to world power was the fact that Romulus and Remus, who found Rome, were suckled by a she-wolf. Which explains pretty cogently how she became a world power and held it in her iron-clad thrall.

However, despite the breakneck speed at which the Romans made the Holy Roman Empire, as it was known, it didn't happen overnight, so to speak. Hence the well-known phrase or saying: 'Rome wasn't built in a day'. Which is not an overly intelligent saying, if I may say so, seeing as obviously Rome wasn't built in a day. No city could be built in a day. Even Milton Keynes, which is the most advanced city in the world and was built entirely by a computer, took two and a half weeks. So clearly, Rome, which was bigger than Manchester, could never, in a month of Sundays, get built in a day!

Pompeii was destroyed in an afternoon, but that's a different story.

So What Was the Roman Dress Like?

The Romans wore long white bath-towels, covering everything fortunately,[1] which was called togas (from Latin *toga* = long white bath-towel). Obviously not everyone wore togas, seeing as they was an insignia of rank. Soldiers and slaves wore tunics, to denote their subsidiary status, which were generally worn well above the knee, although they wore stout underpants underneath, so as not to offend Roman matrons as they bent over to pick up their shopping or whilst climbing into chariots.

Roman Matron

1. Except for one shoulder which was bare.

Roman slave (note tunic)

So Why Did the Romans Wear Togas and Tunics?

The reason the Romans wore togas and tunics, according to historians of the time, was because it was very hot and trousers would have been uncomfortable, although this argument hardly holds water if one looks at modern-day Italy, where you don't get bank managers and policemen and people walking about in tunics. It may be hot, but they wear ordinary long trousers like everyone else. Possibly trousers hadn't been invented, although one can hardly see why it would have been so difficult if they'd already invented viaducts and central heating. What's a pair of trousers to a nation who build the Colossus of Rhodes and the Sistine Chapel? Probably the main reason why Romans wore bath-towels was because they was generally obsessed by cleanliness (like modern-day Swedes), and for this reason built numerous baths wherever possible. These were called *Roman baths*. They were not like the baths in our modern-day bathrooms, however, but instead were like railway stations full of endless swimming pools.

Was There Any Famous Romans?

Yes, there was numerous very famous Romans. In fact the Romans had probably more famous Romans per *capita* than *any other Civilization we've yet had*. Julius Caesar was probably the most well-known famous Roman, who ruled for most of its history. After he was murdered by the Senate (an early version of the House of Commons) Rome went to the dogs, basically, and was ruled by Caligula, who was off his trolley, as his name implies, and Nero, who was worse. Another famous Roman was Hannibal, who was the first man to cross the Alps on an elephant and built Hadrian's Wall.

Julius Caesar

Conclusion

And so we leave Rome at the height of her power with the world still held in her tight-fisted grip. Rome was also famous for the Roman Forum, Billingham Forum[1] and *Ben Hur* which is universally acknowledged as the finest motion picture ever made in the entire history of Man.

THINGS TO DO

1. Make a Roman Candle.

1. Also Blandford Forum.

CHAPTER XIX

The Discovery of Time

'And stands the church clock at ten to three?'
(Lady Jane Grey)

O NE of the most important discoveries of the Romans
was time. In fact before the Romans, people were all
over the place. There were no hours or minutes, no
concept of lunch or tea-time and of course no such thing
as diaries or wall planners. I mean there was time,
obviously, otherwise everything would never have begun,
in other words, it was always there, but no one *knew* it was.
Like electricity or leather.

THINGS TO DO

1. Visit a well-known clock.

CHAPTER XX

The Medes and Persians

'Of al the floures in the Mede
Thanne love I most thise floures white and rede,
Swiche as men callen daysyes in our town.'
(G. Chaucer) [1]

THE Medes and Persians were a very famous desert people who came after the Romans and lived in the desert although they also came before the Romans, as well, as it happens, and had numerous wars with the celebrated Greek, Alfred the Great. He often defeated them, although they often defeated *him* and are in fact the main reason he burnt the cakes, which he done shortly before his death in the Battle of Marathon, celebrated to this day in the Annual London Marathon. [2]

Lobsters

The Kings of the Medes and Persians was Cyrus the Great, then Darius the Great, then Xerxes the Great, then Catherine the Great, all of whom looked identical apart from their hats. The great Persian Kings ruled the earth and were worshipped as gods. This was partly because of

1. Chaucer was a successful novelist, as is well known, so how he got away with disgraceful spelling such as the above is astonishing! For some reason schools in them days paid little or no attention to simple grammar – probably owing to all the numerous invasions going on all the time.

2. To raise money for London charities, such as hospitals etc. Although so many people finish up in hospital as a result that it slightly defeats the object in my opinion.

their charismatic and magnetic personalities and partly because non-worshippers were impaled on spikes and fed to Persian mosquitoes the size of lobsters. The Great King would sit on a throne moulded in the shape of a lion's head with emeralds for eyes and lapis lazuli for teeth. It was made of beaten gold and raised on the skulls of conquered warriors between brassières of burning sandals.

From left to right: Cyrus the Great, Darius the Great,
Xerxes the Great, Catherine the Great

Lingerie

A crucial feature of the Mede and Persian world was that men and women were strictly separated, which is a central reason why the population dropped dramatically. The women lived in the harem and lounged on silk cushions in transparent lingerie sipping sherbert and sweet tea while the men wandered about beating each other's brains out.

**IMPORTANT WARNING
FOR ALL TEACHERS**

**THE REST OF THIS CHAPTER
CONTAINS EXPLICIT SEXUAL
REFERENCES AND ON NO
ACCOUNT SHOULD BE
VIEWED BY PUPILS BELOW
THE AGE OF EIGHTEEN.**

THANK YOU - AUTHOR.

When it was discovered, however, that babies come through sexual conjugations, as it were, and not just out of the blue on a Persian carpet, husbands and wives were allowed to meet once a year in order to do the necessary proclivities – although always under the strict supervision of three elderly lady magi who was there to keep pleasure down to a minimum and generally take notes. Even to me – a strict celibate (for religious reasons) – this would seem an unjustifiably severe moral code to have *within the matrimonial home*. Particularly for newly-weds. A point noted by the well-known sexual expert Sir Sigmund Freud[1] (*see illustration below*).

Freud discovering a Matrimonial Disorder

Conclusion

And so the mighty Medes and Persians pass on down the misty corridors of history.

---

1. In his popular yet controversial works *Your Dreams Foretold* and *Hypnotise your Friends* by Sigmund Freud.

POPULAR MEDE AND PERSIAN
MISCONCEPTIONS NO. I

*Fig 1. Baby being born to a recently married
Mede and Persian couple*

THINGS TO DO

1. Write a powerfully erotic historical novel entitled *The Slave Girl and the Magus* or *A Hot Night in the Harem*.

2. See the popular film *The Knight's Tale* by Geoffrey Chaucer, starring the celebrated Australian actor and model Keith Ledger and one of this country's up and coming young starlets Rufus Sewell.

3. Build a Mede.

CHAPTER XXI

The Rise of Babylon

Q: *Babylonian housewife went to pay her taxes. She had five pounds in one ear and a pound note in the other. What was she?*
A: *Six pounds in arrears.*
(Famous Babylonian Joke)

The Rise of Babylon

BABYLON was the next major Civilization and was chiefly famous for its Hanging Gardens. Unfortunately, however, these were hard to reach due to the fact that they were hanging and cost a fortune to maintain. Nevertheless they were renowned throughout the horticultural world and people still wonder how on earth they did them.

Structure of Society

Needless to say only the Babylonian nobles could afford a hanging garden, though many of the less well-off had little hanging patios, while the slave classes were allowed their own hanging allotments which they dug at weekends when they weren't watering the Hanging Gardens.

Other Attractions

Other attractions were the Lion's Den, the Fiery Furnace and Belshazzar's Feast, which was held weekly.

The End of Babylon

Unfortunately, although Babylon was a gardener's paradise, she was also the Mother of Harlots and every Abomination of the Earth and for this reason was tied to a millstone and cast in the sea by a mighty angel and was found no more.

THINGS TO DO

1. Construct your own Hanging Garden (see easy-to-follow instructions opposite). Amaze your neighbours. Make them GREEN with envy!

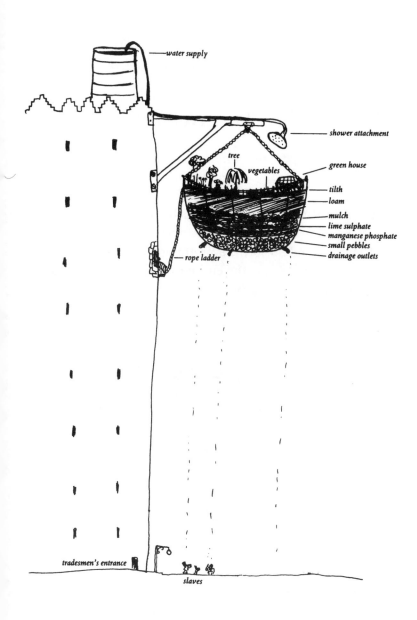

water supply

shower attachment

green house

tree

vegetables

tilth

loam

mulch

lime sulphate

manganese phosphate

small pebbles

drainage outlets

rope ladder

tradesmen's entrance

slaves

Fig 1: The Hanging Gardens of Babylon
(Note massive hanging baskets in which the gardens was hung.)

73

CHAPTER XXII

The Fall of the Roman Empire

'Cocker the clinkie afore the winkie.'
(Unknown)

MEANWHILE in Rome, which everyone had forgotten about due to the Medes and Persians and Mother of Harlots and so forth, everything started going to pot suddenly. Within days the entire Roman Empire had gone rapidly downhill and by the end of the week was completely out of hand. For this reason they decided to have the Fall of the Roman Empire as soon as possible.

Simon Schramrama

Trafalgar Square

Recognized by historians such as Simon Scharmarama[1] as one of the nastiest and most unpleasant incidents in history, the Fall of the Roman Empire astounded the

1. In my view probably the greatest historian of this or any other age.

entire world who was rocked to its foundations. The closest modern parallel to would be a compulsory New Year's Eve party in Trafalgar Square, full of two hundred and fifty thousand Scottish football supporters, all violently drunk and being sick everywhere, going on without pause for six weeks with no toilet facilities. It featured of course in the world-famous endless novel of the same name by Stanley Gibbons and was filmed with a glittering bevy of international celebrities such as Sir Alec Guinness, Dame Sophia Loren and Omar Sharif, the renowned actor and sherrif.

Terrifying

Immediately and with virtually no warning whatsoever, a new kind of people, more terrifying than any previous kind of people, swept through a Europe still covered in bits of old Roman pillars and busts. These were the dreaded Barbarians, also known as Goths or Vandals, under their leader Attila the Hun, the famous hun.

Dame Sophia Loren and Omar Sharif in
The Fall of the Roman Empire

Goths or Vandals

So what kind of people was the Goths or Vandals precisely? Well the Vandals spent their days vandalizing everything (hence their name obviously) while the Goths did exactly the same but wore tattoos, dyed black hair and cheap silver nose rings. In other words, they didn't give a toss about anything and spent the next nine hundred years looting Roman villas, despoiling Roman baths, chasing Roman matrons and knocking down Hadrian's Wall.

Conclusion

For this reason the lights started going out all over Europe. Hence it became known as the Dark Ages.

THINGS TO DO

1. Would you be **(a)** A Goth or a Vandal or **(b)** A Roman Matron or **(c)** neither. Give your reasons.

2. Re-build Hadrian's Wall.

CHAPTER XXIII

The Dark Ages

*'It often shows a fine command of language
to say nothing.'*
(Celestial Seasonings Herb Teas)

THUS it was that the Dark Ages covered the Earth, about which nothing are known, seeing as no-one said much due to the lights being out. The truth is that very little happened in the Dark Ages. With Attila the Hun and all the Goths or Vandals riding about in their nose rings mugging everybody, the best thing was to keep your head down, which is what most people did. They lived in little daub and wattle huts, had babies, visited the neighbours occasionally and died. And that was life in the Dark Ages.

Attila the Hun

Apart from the glorious Byzantine Empire in the East which was famous for its icons and emperors with rectangular heads.

THINGS TO DO

1. Make a little daub and wattle hut (*see easy-to-follow instructions below*):

   a. Make daub

   b. Mix wattle

   c. Erect little hut

   d. Put in little tables and chairs

   e. Put up little pictures

   f. Arrange little ornaments.

CHAPTER XXIV

Monastic Life

'One monk is a monk too many.'
(Viking catch phrase)

THE only people, in fact, who done anything useful at this time was the monks, who risked life and limb illuminating gospels in the Outer Hebrides. Although these took centuries to do because everything was so dark and most of them was half blind anyway, seeing as they worked too close to the page.

Monks in the Outer Hebrides

One of the most famous illuminated gospels was *The Book of Kells*,[1] which had over seven hundred monks

---

1. The Vikings sold *The Book of Kells*, which was useless to them seeing as you couldn't eat it, to Trinity College Dublin for a Friesian bull, six bags of maize and a Danish pastry. It is still there to this day and is very beautiful, obviously, seeing as that's all the monks did all day, although the last pages are in a terrible state, seeing as they was all blind by this time and fumbling about all over each other's pages.

working on it twenty-four hours a day. They done it for three hundred years and had just reached the Flight into Egypt when they was all massacred by the Vikings, who suddenly appeared out of nowhere and are the next major people after the Dark Ages as we shall see.

And so the Dark Ages came to an end. And about time too, in many people's opinions.

THINGS TO DO

1. Illuminate a famous gospel.

2. Appear out of nowhere as a Viking.

3. Come to an end.

CHAPTER XXV

The Vikings – Scourge of Europe

'We're bjord with our fjord.'
(Eric Bloodaxe)

THE Vikings are celebrated for their massacres and pillaging which they done not only to monks but also to everyone else, as is well known. This was mainly due to the fact that they lived in Scandinavia. Seeing as Scandinavia is appallingly cold with about one and a half weeks of daylight a year and the Vikings were cooped up for months on end in their huts, full of goats, hens, babies and the in-laws, they became incredibly aggressive for obvious reasons.

Viking

Viking Home Life

Vikings lived in huts which were earthen mounds covered in bits of old goat skin with a thin layer turf on the roof which they put their cows on. This was a thoughtless and often dangerous practice, however, seeing as the cows, not surprisingly, fell *through* the roof and thus through the ceiling, which played havoc with the milk yield, seeing as the Viking cow lived in a state of more or less permanent anxiety with regard to the stability of his grazing.

The Vikings, therefore, had very little milk. Not only because of the collapsing roof syndrome but also because of the Viking grass which is known, of course, to this day, as tundra (Old Norse: *tun* = grossly inedible grass; *dra* = like old lino). The closest relative to tundra in this country being the astro turf which they put under the fruit displays in greengrocers.

The Runes

It is hardly surprising, therefore, that the Vikings went off and pillaged everywhere, with all the pent-up rage that was penting up during the endless Arctic winters due to collapsing roofs and calcium deficiency and with nothing to do all day except throw Rune stones which were like the I Ching, only worse.

The I Ching

The I Ching is the famous mystic book of Chinese prophecy by which you can see into the future and which I have personally studied in great detail. I know many people find this ancient work a source of great wisdom, but I'm afraid I have to say I find the whole thing somewhat overrated, due to the fact that it tends to be hopelessly unspecific in its replies. For instance, you may ask: 'Should I give the outside of the house a new coat of Sandtex this year or should I leave it until next year?' The answer to this question will probably be something like:

'The storm that covers the goose drowns the rabbit.'

Now fair enough. I can interpret this, after three or four hours of close scrutiny, seeing as I have the mystic training and was in fact once a Chinese monk in the Fifth Dynasty (see Chapter XIV, p. 35, 'Reincarnation') but to the average common-or-garden man-in-the-street, who just wants to know whether to slap a coat of Sandtex up or not, it leaves a lot to be desired.

The I Ching can also be extremely depressing. 'Should I have a boiled egg or All-Bran for breakfast?' could well receive the reply:

'The river breaks its banks and kills all the inhabitants.'

which could put you off breakfast for good.

The Runes

Mind you, compared with the Viking Runes, the I Ching is a day out at Butlin's.[1] The Rune Stones, in fact, are probably the most depressing clairvoyant aid the world has ever known. They come in a small velvet maroon bag with an accompanying booklet and here are some of the so-called ancient insights they have to offer:

'You are stuck in a deep rut.'

'You seek only your own glory and lust after the world's riches'.

'You put yourself alway before the needs of another.'

'You have covered your head in a heavy sack.'

Which are very stupid, not to say irresponsible things to say to someone who might well be in an impression-able state. Particularly someone they've never even met! I have, in fact, written to the publisher of this particular item (*not* Mr Herm I'm very happy to say, who would never get himself mixed up in this kind of mumbo-jumbo) suggest-ing that they take them immediately off the bookstalls as they could easily get into the hands of youngsters or people with low self-esteem who might start taking them seriously. Obviously, I didn't draw these particular runes from the bag *personally*. I just happened to notice them, *en passant* as it were, during my researches. Anyway, I wouldn't have believed them even if I had drawn them.

---

1. The world-famous Holiday Camp. And home, of course, of the popular 'Red Coats' (see Chapter XLVII, 'The American War of In-dependence', page 153).

Modern Scandinavia

Nowadays, of course, the Scandinavians have pine furniture and saunas, every fourth person you meet is an architect, and disease has been eliminated. However, despite these benefits they are generally a gloomy people probably due to the genetic memory of runes, tundra and anxious cows. So much so that the word 'joke' is unknown in Scandinavian. As are 'laughter', 'Brighton Pier', 'punch-line' and Les Dennis. In fact, the only entertainers in Scandinavian showbiz history, apart from the Smurfs and Hedda Gabler, was Abba, the famous singing duo.

Constantly Depressed

Indeed, a quick look at other famous Swedes and Danes will show you how constantly depressed they are. Ingrid Bergman, the famous film director, makes films about death, medieval plagues and crumbling marriages, while Henry Ibsen and Henry Chekhov, the famous Norwegian play-writing team, wrote obsessively about incestuous ornithologists and forest clearance.

Ibsen and Chekhov discussing their latest play

Hygiene

Nevertheless, the Scandinavians are a deeply hygienic race and visitors to Denmark will immediately recall the famous Copenhagen Launderette Riots that brought the city to its knees in 1951. All their toilets smell like pine forests which is very laudable, but I have to admit that I find their use of recycled toilet paper a little hard to handle.

The End of the Vikings

The Vikings all swept over to England but swiftly died out fortunately after eating Alfred's cakes. Numerous Viking words still remain in the English language: they include 'victim', 'viscount', 'vicar' and Queen Victoria.

THINGS TO DO

1. Make a Viking hut with a turf roof. Put a cow on it. Stand clear.

2. Build a Viking ship. Sail to warmer climes. Pillage the local community.

Viking skip

CHAPTER XXVI

The Normans

Q: *A Norman housewife went to pay her taxes. She had five pounds in one ear and a pound note in the other. What was she?*
A: *Six pounds in arrears.*
(Famous Norman Joke)

AFTER the Vikings was the Normans and for this reason England became Norman. In other words everyone was Norman normally, except for the Saxons who were Saxon. Naturally, most people preferred to be Norman seeing as you got your own Motte and Bailey and were allowed to flog the Saxons whenever possible.

New Zealand

One fascinating little-known fact about the Normans is that they were not in fact Normans, but French! And came originally from Calais and Boulogne, which are two of the dullest towns the world has ever known, so it's hardly surprising that they moved to England under the major Norman, William, who was also called the Conqueror, seeing as he beat Harold Nicholson at Hastings, the attractive family resort on the south coast. After him come William II, William III, William IV, William V, William Rufus,[1] William and Mary, and William of Orange, all of whom continued the Norman conquest to the four corners of the world. We know this by all the Hastings

---

1. Intriguingly the same name exactly as Rufus Sewell the popular actor.

there are everywhere. There is a Hastings in Nebraska and one in Michigan and, most astounding of all, one in New Zealand. As well as a New Brighton and a Nelson, which is pretty conclusive evidence that the Normans invaded New Zealand too.

Aku Aku

It is also my surmise that the seven hundred stone gods on Aku Aku, the famous Easter Island, are in fact wearing Norman helmets and are *none other* than Norman monarchs. And how come you get *sheriffs* as far afield as Nottingham, America and Arabia (e.g. Omar Sharif)? Surely this is simply *more incontestable evidence* that the Normans didn't just beat England at the Battle of Hastings but virtually every country in the entire world.

Famous Norman Things

The Normans, of course, were famous for various famous things such as Norman arches, Norman wisdom and Norman hair, which was the shortest the world had yet seen. Their main claim to fame, however, was the celebrated *Doomsday Book*, which had everyone in England in it and was colossally big for this reason. It took four hundred oxen to drag it from town to town, so they could write down everyone's name, address and mother's maiden name (for security purposes).

Straight to Paperback

Despite its size, the *Doomsday Book* was very popular, particularly at Christmas, when sales were astronomical. It went straight into paperback and became a world bestseller. The main problem with it, of course, was that no sooner was it published than it was out of date, particularly with regard to the Saxons, who were permanently escalating the population after dark in their hovels.

Norma Major

Famous Normans

The Normans was also famous for many famous Normans, such as Norman Hartnell, Norman Bates, Barry Norman and Norma Major.

Famous Norman Kings

But probably the Normans was most famous for their famous Norman kings, such as Richard the Lionheart, who died in battle, and King John, who died in the Wash. In fact ninety per cent of all Norman kings died. Apart from Henry V who beat the pathetic and weak French under their corrupt and decadent King Dauphin, who had tragically thin legs and black tights and was like a very thin version of Richard III but without the hunch. He was very cruel to his people and is famous for burning Joan of Arc, due to her voices.

Louis XIV

In fact all French monarchs are famous for their cruelty and decadence, especially Louis XIV the famous French king and Marie Antoinette his wife, a jumped-up interior decorator from Rheims who spent the entire French budget on shoes and dressing-tables. They then proceeded to alienate the entire French peasantry by dressing up as simulated shepherds and frolicking about with the French nobility, who wore wigs and beauty spots and spent their time running the peasants over in their carriages. For this reason the peasants rose with their pitchforks, invented the guillotine and killed everyone with a wig or a beauty spot, which wasn't particularly surprising but was a little hard on people with toupées and moles, obviously.

French Revolution

This period is known as the French Revolution, and is remembered chiefly, of course, for the Scarlet Pimpernel, who was actually an Englishman and whose memory lives on in the legendary English flower that was named after him. It is small and red, as was he. He dressed up as old women and railway porters and his daring exploits often involved the aristocracy dressing up as old women and railway porters too. This many of them refused to do, however, because old women's and railway porters' clothes tended to be very smelly.

The Scarlet Pimpernel leading the disguised French Aristocracy through customs.

THINGS TO DO

1. Make a scale model of **either** Aku Aku **or** Nottingham.

2. Conduct the French Revolution.

3. Dress up as **one** of the following: **(a)** a simulated shepherd **(b)** a railway porter **(c)** Norma Major.

CHAPTER XXVII

Modern France

'France c'est moi.'
(Anatole France)

AFTER the French Revolution, the French coat-of-arms was changed to a woman standing in the wind and, to this day, France is a changed nation and everybody is very happy. Apart from that, nothing has happened in French history of any major significance.

Eiffel Tower

France is famous for the Eiffel Tower, the hunchback of Notre Dame and the giant hypermarket at Dunkirk, whose cheese counter alone is approximately a mile and a half long, while famous French inventions include French letters, French fries and French Windows.[1]

Fin de Siècle

France more or less came to an end at the end of the *Fin de Siècle*, but this we shouldn't hold against them.[2]

---

1. French Windows have revolutionized the modern living-room throughout the world – seeing as without them it would still be virtually impossible to step straight on to our patio or lawns.

2. I am of course *fully* aware that I have slightly strayed from the strictly chronological at this juncture. Needless to say, this is entirely intentional and isn't because 'I'm losing my grip' actually, Raymond. It is in fact an example of what is technically known as a 'tangent' and is what many leading authors go off at in order to make numerous crucial points that they couldn't have made if they hadn't gone off at it. As a matter of interest it is generally agreed that tangents are

Eiffel Tower

THINGS TO DO

1. Write a French letter.

probably the single most important innovation in the modern novel today. In fact I happen to know that the panel of judges for the Booker Prize, who probably know more about the art of writing than most people, has recently sent out a memo throughout the literary world requesting a greater use of tangents generally.

CHAPTER XXVIII

The Fourteenth Century

'Lay you wame to your weft and skirkit your cleft.'
(Fourteenth-century proverb)

IMMEDIATELY after the Normans came the four-teenth century, which is one of the most famous centuries in the world. It is chiefly famous for two things which are as follows.

Courtly Love

Courtly Love was when you wrote ballads and went jousting for a fine Lady, but couldn't do anything, if you get my meaning. You could to your wife, obviously, but she wasn't your Lady. Your wife was just ordinary, who you did the hoovering with and so forth. Your Lady, on the other hand, was beyond compare, unblemished as snow and you would crawl through nettles stark naked, or anything else she requested, just so as you could hold her hanky.

A Lady Beyond Compare

Hanky

You put the hanky on your lance, generally. If you had one. Some knights had quite a big lance, which tended to be extremely popular with the ladies, while other knights had little lances and found it quite a problem finding a Lady at all.

Black Death

The second thing it is chiefly famous for was the Black Death, in which you started off with a slight headache and finished up writhing in agony and covered in boils. Basically the Black Death come from the fact that people chucked all their plate scrapings and buckets of slops and everything into the streets or worse, into the house opposite,[1] which wasn't difficult seeing as fourteenth-century houses were generally only inches apart. Which means that everyone got everyone else's slops all the time. As they do in fact to this day in many modern camp sites.

How Many Died?

All in all, three people in every one died of the Black Death. At one point there wasn't anyone in Europe left at all. Just a load of empty countries and piles of dirty plates and sewage everywhere. If you was to imagine Hay-on-Wye on a Sunday morning, with half the sewage of Bombay piled up down the street, that was Europe at the time of the Black Death.

---

1. Including, to be perfectly candid, their personal waste or 'toiletry' deposits, if you get my meaning, of which I need say no more, except that there would have been an appalling load, due to their massive families, owing to the total lack of birth control, except for the rhythm method and dock leaves.

Witchcraft

The Fourteenth Century was also famous for its witches, who were generally in charge of medieval community health care and were the equivalent to our modern-day local GP, although they were a bit harder to find, seeing as they generally lived in a fetid hovel in the middle of a dark forest with a couple of ravens or an owl. They continued more or less unabated until doctors were finally introduced by the National Health Service, which came in under Sir Thomas Beecham in 1948.

Other Important Developments

The fourteenth century was also famous for acorns, steeple hats and numerous popular tortures.

THINGS TO DO

1. Choose from the following numerous popular Fourteenth-Century tortures you would have chosen if you had the choice:

    (a) Sheridan's Pilliwinks

    (b) Spencer's Gyves

    (c) Billington's Trousers.

    (d) Benedict's Balls.

2. Fashion a noble and mighty sword from living steel, with a blade as true and straight as any in all England.

CHAPTER XXIX

The Thirteenth Century

'A man with an oyster is worth two with a broom.'
(Nostradamus)

MEANWHILE before the Fourteenth Century they had the Thirteenth Century which was probably almost as famous as the Fourteenth Century seeing as they had the Crusades which lasted for six hundred years. These were fought in Constantinople, which was in fact Rome until it was re-named Constantinople so as to avoid capture. For this reason it kept moving about, which is why the war[1] went on for so long because nobody knew where it was at any given time.

Street Clearance

It did, however, give the Pope a chance to clear up the streets of Rome after the Fall of the Roman Empire and shift all the broken pillars and rotting fruit and so forth so as he could get Roman Catholicism off the ground. This street clearance, or 'Rome Improvement' as it became known, was mainly done by the Swiss Guard who wear short skirts and pom-poms and are extremely clean, like all Swiss people. Not as clean as the Swedes, obviously, but still very hygienic. No doubt the holy Pontiff would have had the Swedes in, except they was still Vikings and therefore pagan.

---

1. Also known as the Wars of the Roses, the Hundred Years War, the War of Jenkins Ear and the War of the Worlds.

The Pope

Appalling Paganism

In fact due to the appalling paganism still going on everywhere, the Pope sent out numerous well-known saints such as St Patrick, St Augustus and St Benedictine to combat the endless heathens who still believed in corn dollies and curing warts with dandelions and so forth.

Very Handy

To aid them in their tasks, of course, many of the saints were allowed to perform miracles, which must have come in very handy if you was doing a conversion, particularly of an entire pagan people. St Patrick, for instance, rid the whole of Ireland of snakes and as a result thousands of great hairy lager-swilling Vikings became devout churchgoers overnight.[1]

Saints

As a general principal, all saints had to be a patron saint of one thing and you pray to them depending on what it is:

1. As a result, St Patrick was approached by many other countries, such as India, Australia and South America, who offered sole and unconditional conversion rights in repayment for the total abolition of all snakes, spiders, piranhas etc. Patrick, however, would never leave his native Ireland, which is why those countries are still so appallingly full of snakes, insects, sharks, etc.

St Bernard for mountain rescue, St Bruno for pipes, St Pancras for railways, St Michael for underwear, St Catherine for wheels and St Valentine for obvious reasons.

Some Famous Saints

St Augustus   *St Patrick*   *St Benedictine*   *St Bruno*

And so it was that the sun set on the mighty Thirteenth Century – without which who knows where we'd have been.

THINGS TO DO

Write short notes on at least **four** of the following:

(a) pom-poms;

(b) Swedes;

(c) warts.

CHAPTER XXX

The Story of St Francis

'Fair stood the wind for Francis.'
(Anon)

PROBABLY the most renowned saint, however, was St Francis of Assisi, who was the rich son of a medieval cloth merchant who one day give all his father's cloth to beggars, which didn't please his father, obviously. Or indeed the beggars. Who now had to wander the plague-infested back streets of Renaissance Italy with their prams not only full of old newspapers and fire-grates but also great twenty-foot bales of heavy curtain material.

For this reason, St Francis was publicly beaten by his father, so he cut a tonsure on his head and went about the land preaching to all the animals. And the animals stopped whatever they was doing, and sat by St Francis and quietly listened to him. And the birds, too, and the fishes. And even the trees also. And as a result of having heard his words, the birds sang in the air and the fish sang in the sea and the flowers sang in their fields and the moles sang in their burrows.

The Famous Wolf of Gubbio Story

And a wolf was killing sheep and terrifying the attractive Italian village of Gubbio which was trying to destroy it and thus advertising for a knight. So St Francis came and said 'I will go.' So he went. And they said, 'Take with you a sword'; and he said 'No.' And he went in his habit and his tonsure and he found the wolf in his lair and the wolf was snarling but Francis went in.

The animals listen to St Francis

And the people waited behind their walls and Francis did not return and the red sun was just sinking below the Umbrian hills when they spied through the olive groves a man walking with a wolf wagging his tail. (The wolf wagging his tail, obviously, not Francis.) And the wolf lay at his feet and let them stroke him and the people let him lick their hand and the wolf stayed in the village and became their friend, and St Francis said, 'There is no need for fear no more'.

And he went up a hill and became older than he'd ever been or would ever be again and saw a six-winged Seraph[1] and immediately understood everything as clear as a bell and saw to the bottom of the depths of all in-finity, and stood on the head of a pin and saw the universe in a raindrop, and totally knew the answer to every question that had ever been asked. And he saw life as a tiny little closed potting shed inside a wondrous eternal garden. And realized that all human anxiety was but a single pebble in the ocean.

1. Six-winged Seraph = an extremely high-up angel with six wings.

The End of Francis

And he lay there for six days and for six nights and was nearly frozen solid and the monks come and took him home and he sang and smiled and said: 'I have been there, sunshine.' And just before he died they got him a load of blankets and ermine and hot-water bottles and a jewelled fur hat and so on because his body shivered greatly. And they also got him a load of biscuits and buns and cakes as a last treat, because they loved him.

But St Francis said, 'No, no, carry me and put me on the cold night earth without any clothes or cakes or buns or anything. Put me beneath the stars into the hearts of which I have journeyed when I was up the hill.' So they placed him naked on the naked ground and they stood with him and watched. And little animals crept up too and watched also. And owls. And the wolf. And they all said goodbye.

And that was the story of Francis of Assisi.

THINGS TO DO

1. See if there is a nearby town or village where an untamed pet is dangerously rampant from lack of self-esteem. Go there, unarmed, and talk to the animal.

2. Build the Doge of Venice.

CHAPTER XXXI

The Renaissance

*'The next major thing that occurred after
the Normans was the Renaissance, as is well known.'*
(D. Dingle)

IMMEDIATELY after the Normans, the next major thing to occur was the Renaissance. The reason it was called the Renaissance, of course, was all the famous statues, buildings and music, which was done at the time, such as the *Mona Lisa*, *Wuthering Heights* and Mozart's *Moonlight Sonata*, without whom the world would never be the same again and were chiefly the result of Queen Elizabeth I, who started the Renaissance off single-handed, so to speak, and is therefore the most famous monarch of all time, as is our own Queen today, obviously.

Housewife and Monarch

For this reason the Renaissance is popularly known across the world as the Age of Elizabeth. Or the Elizabethan Age. Unfortunately, Queen Elizabeth I – unlike our own Queen, who clearly delights in her joint role as housewife and monarch – never married or sired an heir. Not, obviously, because she wasn't a very attractive woman which she clearly was (maybe not everyone's cup of tea but certainly nothing out of place, if you get my meaning) but so as she could devote her entire life to patronising the arts and go on tour with various theatre companies.

Philip II

Animal Urges

It is ironic that Elizabeth I came closest to marriage when she met the suave, charming and recklessly good-looking Philip II of Spain (*see above*). After going out with him for a few years, she finally chose to put the Renaissance before her animal urges. But if she hadn't and had married him, then her husband would have been called Philip too, exactly like our own Queen's is. A fascinating coincidence of history that didn't come to pass but could have.

Breakthroughs in Art

The Renaissance was chiefly responsible for numerous breakthroughs in art. One of the most famous break-throughs, in some cases literally, was the art of perspective, in which artists started doing paintings of distance that were so realistic that people felt you could walk into them. In fact many Renaissance paintings were ruined because members of the public kept walking straight through them, thinking it was a real landscaped garden or canal.

Brass Knobs

This is why many art galleries introduced the brass-knobbed posts and white rope barriers that are still in use to this day. They have also been introduced into many banks, building societies and Post Offices, as it happens, although, of course, this has nothing to do with the art of perspective, obviously, but the parlous state of present-day queueing which unfortunately is not what it used to be, since we opened our ports to all and sundry tourists, who just start pushing in willy-nilly the moment they see a cashier.

The Mona Lisa

The famed painting by Leonardo da Vinci,
The Anaconda Smile *has mystified and intrigued art-lovers for centuries. Stand this open page on the mantelpiece and observe how she follows you about the room.*

The Male Nude

Another breakthrough was the male nude. Before the Renaissance no-one painted men nude. They painted women nude, obviously, but not men and if they did paint men nude they was always covered by a leaf or vine. Suddenly, however, Renaissance painters and decorators just started showing men totally nude with nothing on. For this reason many people, mainly women, but also some men who had never dared look, were deeply shocked and fainted when they saw these male nudes, seeing as they often didn't know that what men have there is there, thinking that men have leaves or vines permanently where they in fact have their parts.

The Male Nude during the Renaissance

The Reformation

Nowadays, of course, we see a statue of a naked man with all his parts showing and no-one bats an eyelid but in those days a man showing all his parts, even in stone or marble, was a deeply shocking experience and many people went around after the Renaissance adding leaves or knocking parts off. This was called the Reformation.

Illicit Proclivities

One of the most famous artists of the time was, of course, Michelangelo, whose most famous work was the Sistine Chapel, and the nude statue of Moses, which he also done. As well as his great works of art, Michelangelo is also celebrated for the amount of self-loathing he achieved on account of him engaging in certain illicit proclivities known today as the Love That Dare Not Speak Its Name. I think I make myself clear. He did not care for the company of women, in other words. In fact, he loathed himself so much on this account that he forced himself to lie on his back day in day out wearing only a loin cloth and paint the Creation. It is hard to believe that the man who done this wouldn't even look in a mirror, so much did he loathe himself on account of his proclivities which are nowadays perfectly normal and is the choice of many people, many of whom are celebrities in all walks of life.

Charlton Heston

Michelangelo was, of course, played by Charlton Heston in the famous film *The Agony and the Ecstasy*. And superbly too, if I may say so. Needless to say, Mr Heston has never needed to engage in the Love That Dare Not Speak Its Name and has a charming wife, a red setter and two delightful children, Frazer and Holly.

★ ★ ★

LITTLE KNOWN FACTS NO. 3

Very few people know that Michelangelo was, in fact, born and bred a mere five minutes from the centre of Bournemouth (*see plate*). His parents left England when he was three to avoid the Black Death and went to Italy which is probably the worst place they could have gone, having probably the worst sanitation of anywhere in Europe, as it still does to this day. Though they couldn't have known that at the time, obviously.

THINGS TO DO

1. Discuss why it was you think the Renaissance died out so suddenly. Was it **(a)** disease; **(b)** climatic catastrophe; **(c)** the critics?

2. Write an essay on **one** of the following:

   (a) sanitation;

   (b) animal urges;

   (c) Charlton Heston;

   (d) Building Societies.

CHAPTER XXXII

The Age of Discovery

'Who travels to Rome returns a Greek.'
(Old Wives' Tale. Meaning unknown)

A FEW weeks after the Renaissance, loads of things started being discovered all over the place. Thus began the Age of Discovery.

An Important Discovery

One of the most important discoveries, of course, was astronomy, and numerous astronomers come to fruition at this time. The most famous of these was Galileo, who had a beard and invented the telescope via which he discovered that the earth goes round the sun. Which meant of course that the sun didn't go round the earth, as was thought previous. Needless to say, this was not warmly received by the Pope, who had just sent out a papal bull saying the opposite, ie that the earth went round the sun and he definitely knew this, seeing as he was Pope. Which meant if it was proved it didn't, he was a ruined man, with nothing but a massive wife, thirty screaming children and a rat-infested hovel on the outskirts of Livorno to look forward to. Being a defrocked Pope in the Renaissance was no laughing matter. It certainly didn't mean a retirement villa and full pension on the holiday Isle of Capri, which defrocked Popes get nowadays.

A New Gadget

And so on 1st October 1621, the Pope asked Galileo round for a drink and showed him an intriguing new gadget that sucks your innards out of your nose for thirty-six days while releasing wild rodents into all your orifices. The following morning Galileo looked through his telescope again and discovered that actually the Sun did go round the Earth after all. He apologized for his error and admitted that he thought it was the Sun he'd seen before whereas actually it was the Earth which looked remarkably similar on that particular day.

Advances in Medicine

Meanwhile there was numerous advances in medicine. Particularly in England where Sir Harvey Nichols had just invented surgery which rapidly caught the imagination of the entire medical profession. So much so that enthusiastic young doctors began doing it on anyone regardless of the ailment. Immediately Renaissance health clinics were crammed with patients eager to go beneath the surgeon's knife though interest tailed off after a few weeks when it was discovered that nobody had invented anaesthetics.[1]

Other Famous Renaissance Doctors and Nurses

Other famous Renaissance doctors and nurses were Florence Nightingale, Doctor Dolittle and Ian Fleming.

---

1. The only form of anaesthetics in the Renaissance was of course the Renaissance bullet which they gave to patients to bite during the operation. The skill of the anaesthetist lay in seeing when the writhing patient had bitten through the bullet and inserting another bullet before the patient bit through his own jaw and often the operating table itself. Employment offices of the time were often full of queues of fingerless Elizabethan anaesthetists.

Papal Bull

THINGS TO DO

1. Practice an early operation on someone of your acquaintance. Make sure you do it **either** with anaesthetics **or** without. Explain why.

2. Play the popular game 'Doctors and Nurses' with a total stranger.

CHAPTER XXXIII

The Age of Shakespeare

*'There is a corner of some foreign field
that is for ever Shakespeare.'*
(Peter Brook)

THE OTHER name given to the Renaissance by modern-day historians[1] is of course the Age of Shakespeare, who was born at more or less this time and is now universally accepted to be not only the most celebrated writer to ever put pen to paper (or quill to parchment to be precise[2]) but also the most famous person who ever lived.

Birth of Shakespeare

William Shakespeare was born in Shakespeare's Birthplace in Stratford-Upon-Avon to his mother Mary Arden, the popular Stratford cosmetics expert. She immediately opened the house to the public which made them an absolute fortune but must have been unsettling to the newly-born babe who spent his formative years mewling and puking at every opportunity. It was there that he met Anne Hathaway, with whom he was to have a stormy and incestuous marriage in later years and who inspired him

---

1. Such as Simon Scharmarama and Mother Julius of Norwich.

2. Obviously not all writers have used pen and ink. The Vikings used whalebone and blubber to write their sagas while the famous Greek dramatists used chisel and stone which is why they only wrote one play every thirty years. It also explains why their plays are so long, seeing as, once written, they were rarely prepared to do re-writes.

to write his three most heartfelt comedies *As You Like It,*
Do You Want It and *There You Have It.*

The Life of Shakespeare

Unfortunately that is all that is known of the colourful
and rumbustious life of William Shakespeare. Apart from
his love affair with a moustached girl who unblocked his
writer's cramp and was made into the film *Shakespeare in*
Love which in my opinion is, after *The Ten Commandments,*
Ben-Hur, Lawrence of Arabia and *Genghis Khan,* certainly
the greatest film ever made since Shakespeare's day.

Shakespeare

An Easy Mistake

Not many people realize that there are not one but two
Stratford-Upon-Avons. One of the Stratford-Upon-Avons
is in Stratford-Upon-Avon while the other Stratford-
Upon-Avon is in Stratford Ontario which is in Canada.
The thing is that both Stratford-Upon-Avons have a
Royal Shakespeare Theatre Company but more important *both towns look virtually identical.* So DO CHECK
your tickets before getting on the train to make sure you're
going to the right one! Many theatre-goers have been

bitterly disappointed to arrive at the theatre only to find they should actually be 8000 miles away.[1]

A Nasty Surprise

However I feel it incumbent upon me not to conclude this chapter without revealing to the reader a very nasty surprise I had recently when I happened to innocently glance at a version of Shakespeare's plays known, for some reason, as the First Folio edition and spelt exactly as Shakespeare wrote it. Obviously I am not at liberty to say where I got my hands on such a document, but I can say that it left me very deeply shocked indeed.

Shocking

For it is written as though by an illiterate four-year-old child. With nearly every word spelt wrong. Not to mention the grammar and punctuation which is all over the place. Fortunately – and in the nick of time, if I may say so – he has been cleaned up and spelt correctly, so the general public is none the wiser. But one can imagine what would happen if the tabloid press got hold of this. *It doesn't bear thinking about!*

---

1. While I have the attention of Canadian readers, I would just like to say 'howdy' to the many new Canadian friends that I will doubtless have made as a result of this mighty tome and to say that I have, in fact, had the enormous privilege of meeting a number of Canadian people in my life, all of whom I have found very interesting in nearly every aspect. Anyway, many of them have told me they feel deprived of all the culture and history of the British Isles of which they was once part. As a result I believe that a cultural lecture tour of 'The Land of Eternal Winter' might help 'bridge the gap' between our nations and if an offer did happen to be forthcoming in this regard I can absolutely guarantee that Raymond and myself would not only be honoured but also available; or if not Raymond, who has his many duties as my assistant and trainee to attend to, I most certainly would, for a reasonable fee obviously, at a couple of days' notice. Please contact Nick Herm Books or, if they're closed, me personally.

Miss Juliet Stevenson

It is a well-known fact that I am an extremely close personal friend of the renowned actress Miss Juliet Stevenson, who, in my opinion, is one of the biggest prima donnas in this country.[1] It has been my deep personal honour to have appeared with her on various academic radio programmes on BBC Radio 4 and upon my humble request she did graciously grant me a five minute in-depth interview with her personally in her most attractive dressing-room suite for exclusive use in this lowly volume.

Ghengis Khan

One of the very many pertinent topics we touched upon was the question of Shakespeare's spelling and grammar, and she personally told me that she is highly relieved that he is now being spelt correctly, even though that's not how he wrote it, otherwise the great actors and actresses of this country, of which she is clearly one and will go a long way, if I may say so, wouldn't understand the half of what he's saying and would simply never learn the lines; and Miss Stevenson has had a few to learn in her time, I can tell you, having played a wide bevy of Shakespearian parts or 'roles' including Juliet, obviously, Isobel, Shylock and Pollyanna.

1. And star of more films than I can possibly mention in this small space, such as *Truly, Deeply, Madly*, *The English Patient*, *Shakespeare in Love* and *Bridge over the River Kwai*.

THINGS TO DO

1. Write this chapter in your own words.

WARNING

DON'T go writing to famous actresses like Miss Stevenson asking for interviews and so forth. She granted one to me seeing as I am a famous author and we have a natural rapport, but most of her day is spent learning lines and giving lectures and so forth. So she has precious little time to answer reams of facile questions from sycophantic fans all day long.

CHAPTER XXXIV

The Life of the Buddha

'I am The Buddha.'
(Buddha)

BUDDHA was a very rich Indian prince who had everything his heart could desire. Fine clothes and turbans, jewels and peacocks, gold howdahs, tandoori cooking and a very rare pet Muntjac deer. But one day his eye fell upon all the suffering people of India who was just wandering about in pain outside the palace walls. Some were in silent twos and threes, many were alone. A few sat on the hard, shadeless mud surrounded by flies and being picked off by snakes, but most just walked around crying to themselves and wondering why they weren't dead.

Buddha Walks the Dusty Roads

And so, despite his parents' entreaties, he left the jewel-encrusted palace and walked the dusty roads of India on his horse. And after seeing all the suffering in the entire world he sat under a bodhi tree and meditated for seventy-five years until his jewellery and ear-rings and ankle-chains and everything fell off and lay about him where he sat, and his very expensive horse hung about waiting to go, got thin and died suddenly under its jewelled saddle. And all the bodhis withered and everything decayed and disintegrated around him while he was just sat there on his own in his loin-cloth, which hadn't disintegrated fortunately, and birds came and nested in his hair, seeing as they thought he was a bush.

Buddha Sat under the Tree

And Buddha, having been sat under this tree for seventy-five years, discovered what it takes a practising Buddhist like me a mere weekend to grasp. Basically that:

1) We must totally *rid ourselves of our egos* (which I have totally succeeded in doing, I'm happy to say).[1]

2) That nothing can actually hurt us seeing as everything doesn't exist anyway so we don't exist so nothing exists seeing as it's all illusion and this is basically the answer to all suffering as we know it today.

Buddha sat under a tree

Buddha Invents Buddhism

And thus it was that Buddha invented Buddhism and helped all the suffering of the world. Buddhists nowadays wear orange robes and have bald heads so as to deter birds from nesting on them when they meditate.

---

1. In fact a number of well-known Buddhist monks have told me that, of all the people they've known, I have lost my ego more fully than probably anybody else doing it today.

Buddha and Myself

I would just like to say that as a result of a recent past-life regression hypnosis session, I have evidence that I was once a very big Tibetan Llama which will explain pretty categorically how I know so much about this fascinating but complex subject.

THINGS TO DO

1. Become one with the spontaneous non-duality of the moment outside of all ego-concentrated time limitations.

CHAPTER XXXV

Other Major World Philosophies

'Groweth sed and bloweth med,
and springth the wude nu.'
(Unknown)

ANYWAY, besides Buddha, there was also numerous other major spiritual disciplines, such as Taoism, which is Chinese and teaches us to remember we are in tune with the sacred web of the universe and are no different to rivers or mountains or the innocent blades of grass. For instance, if you're an innocent blade of grass and the wind gently waves you and the sun warms you with its rays, you sit there and enjoy it, but if you're trodden on by a boot and crushed underfoot and then it drizzles and you die, you have to lump it like any other blade of grass. Christianity is another famous philosophy, invented by Jesus, of course, and is very similar, as is Hinduism, invented by no-one in particular. All of them says basically the same thing: 'You are not here for why you think you are, you're here for another reason that we are not at liberty to tell you yet.'

THINGS TO DO

1. Become a convert to a famous world religion.

CHAPTER XXXVI

History in the Home

'There are few things better, in my opinion,
than acting out an famous historic event
in your own garden or living-room.'
(Florence Nightingale)

AMONGST many other things, I am probably most famous for my legendary re-enactments of history which have appeared on stage and screen. As a result I have had literally sackfuls of letters from viewers writing to me personally, asking for 'tips from the expert' on how to run their own historical re-enactments in their own homes.

For this reason I have decided to present – as part of this volume and for the first time in a work of such intellectual grandeur – the chance to act out your own historic moments *in your own homes!*

NOW TURN TO PAGE 119!!!

- *FOR A **FULLY ILLUSTRATED** SELECTION OF SUBJECTS*

- *SPECIALLY RESEARCHED **BY THE AUTHOR!!!***

- *A BEVY OF **TIME-SAVING TIPS!!!***

- *SUITABLE FOR **ALL THE FAMILY!!!***

- *GUARANTEED **ENDLESS ENJOYMENT!!!***

- *MAXIMUM **EDUCATIONAL VALUE!!!***

NB All photos guaranteed *actual re-enactments* (no models used)

9. SPARTACUS

The tyrant Crassus repels the gladiatorial hordes of rebel freedom-fighters. Although it is quite possible to re-enact most of the story in a normal self-contained flat or dwelling house, a garden is obviously essential for the bondage scenes in the salt mines and the mass crucifixions at the end. Ideal for all the family.

10. INVASION OF THE VIKINGS!

The gallant Britons defend their homesteads against the dreaded Norsemen. A good one for couples.
N.B. Check with your Insurance Company re. additional premiums for battle re-enactments in the home.
Don't forget that actual burning and pillaging of property, particularly one's own, can be costly
and upset neighbours. See Plate 16 for a real-life example of tragic over-enthusiasm.

11. THE BATTLE OF BALACLAVA

The Heavy Brigade under legendary General Scarlett sweep down from the Fedioukine Heights to meet the crack Russian Dnieper Regiment on the windswept plains of Balaclava. The gallant Scots Greys (left) gallop to the rescue in perfect military formation. While the cruel and scheming Prince Menshikov and his generals (right) look on from the fourth Redoubt. Note the boldly imaginative use of numbers here.

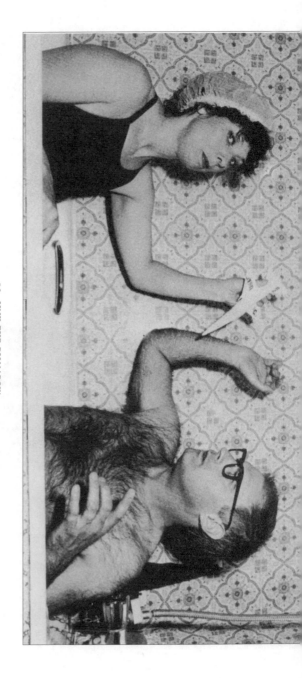

12. SINK THE BISMARCK!

Another excellent re-enactment for couples. Although, needless to say, not the very dubious so-called 'adult-game', common – so I hear – in certain Showbiz parties! Our 'Sink the Bismarck' also happens to take place in the bath and is also played by two adult people but for no other reason than that the bathroom is the most appropriate setting for a naval battle. It would be naïve to suggest that this is a re-enactment for two total strangers but to try and fit more than two adults into the bath would be uncomfortable and upset the manoeuvering of the boats.

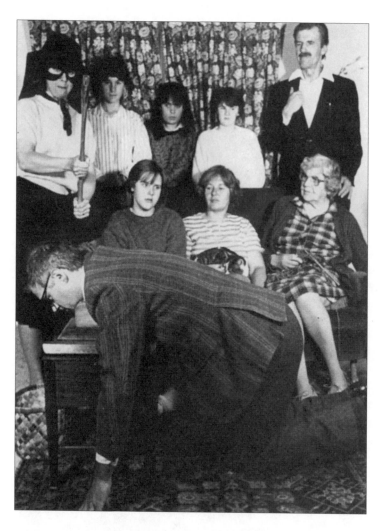

13. EXECUTION OF CHARLES I

*Ideal for dwellings with limited accommodation. Another good one
for all the family and an excellent introduction for friends.*

14a. Don't always go for the leading role! This organiser is in danger of losing the full attention of other participants.

14b. Allot roles with sensitive regard to age and agility. This elderly person certainly has the maturity and no doubt the acting skills to essay the demanding emotional range of Boadicea, but it is unfair to expect her to participate in the strenuous battles, marches and blood-letting rituals that the role necessitates.

15a. Don't be TOO rigid with regard to total historical truth. Be flexible!
Let the Black Prince stand in front of the archers if he wants to.

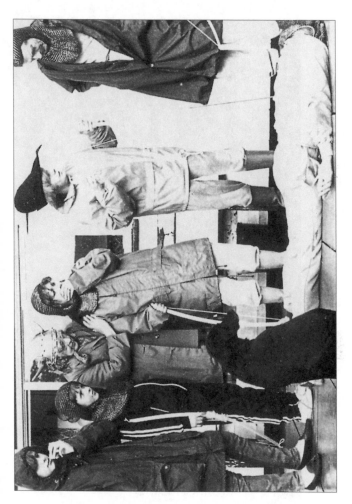

15b. Authenticity isn't everything!

16. WARNING

Be careful! This was the scene after Mr and Mrs Wearn of Epsom had attempted their own re-enactment of World War II. A little bit of care and forethought can save years of subsequent heartache. The Wearns' bill came to £203,000. Mr Wearn lost his job as a Consultant Rot Specialist, Mrs Wearn is in a home and the children, aged 8 and 11, a little boy and girl, are in Council care. History in the Home re-enactments bring families together, not rend them apart!

CHAPTER XXXVII

The British Commonwealth

'This semi-precious jewel,
This infectious breed of Kings.'
(Shakespeare)

AFTER the Elizabethan Age came the Puritans under Oliver Cromwell, who was a Roundhead. Meanwhile Elizabeth's heir, Charles I, was King and led the Cavaliers. Hence they had the Civil War. The reason being was the Roundheads was very stern and wore armour in the house and recycled their waste, while the Cavaliers had long hair, swaggered about and generally chucked everything away regardless.

The Situation Becomes Rapidly Untenable

The situation became rapidly untenable and finally reached breaking point when a group of long-haired Cavaliers started swaggering on a Roundhead's recycled sprouts. There was a furore in the Commons and the following day the Civil War was declared, sweeping through Europe in a matter of minutes.

War Breaks Out

Immediately, the Roundheads turned their pitchforks into ploughshares and marched on Buckingham Palace, which they razed to the ground, although the Royal Family had all gone to Balmoral for their holidays.

Peace Declared

After numerous battles at Edgware Road, Bunkers Hill and Bannockburn, the war came to an end when the Round-heads caught the king hiding up an oak tree, where he was immediately executed via beheading.

King Charles I caught up the oak tree

The Birth of Parliament

Oliver Cromwell – renowned, of course, for his warts and all – then became Prime Minister and invented Parliament. He experimented with various forms of Parliament including the Long Parliament, the Short Parliament, the Rump Parliament and the Addled (or 'smelly') Parliament, before finally settling on The *Houses* of Parliament, which we still have to this day, and Big Ben, of course, the renowned clock.

The British Commonwealth

He is probably most famous, however, for inventing the British Commonwealth (or 'Empire'). Which is famed throughout the world and still pays homage to Her

Majesty who visits it whenever she can with numerous Royal Visits, and gets a very warm welcome whenever she does so obviously.

The Queen visits Australia

But Where Was All the Cavaliers at this Time?

Meanwhile the Cavaliers ran straight off to France, where they carried on swaggering and running over peasants in their carriages until the French Revolution, when all the French Cavaliers (or *Noblesse Oblige*) started getting guillotined so they all swaggered back to England which was in fact the same as it had been before they'd gone, owing to the Restoration, which had come in under Charles II and Nell Gwynn,[1] seeing as Oliver Cromwell had suddenly died of massive sexual repression and his son, Melvin, who succeeded him as Lord Protector of All England and the Commonwealth, wasn't really suitable, being more interested in karaoke.

1. The popular orange seller and mistress.

The Monarch and the PM Nowadays

Fortunately, the Monarch and the PM nowadays are no longer at war and are very good friends. They in fact know each other socially, often go on holiday together and buy each other Christmas presents and so on. So although the Prime Minister makes the actual laws of the country, in other words makes the decisions that affect our day-to-day living – whether to have more battleships, for instance; where to have new traffic lights and so on – he will always check it out with the Monarch first. This happens in the famous Monday meetings at Buckingham Palace, when the PM and the entire House of Commons supplicate themselves on the floor of the throne room and report to Her Majesty all the new Acts of Parliament that they are hoping to be making.

Parliament supplicating themselves before the monarch

Only Too Keen to Help

Obviously, if the Monarch radically objected to a particular Act, they wouldn't pass it, but this is incredibly rare because a Monarch such as ours is only too keen to help in the running of the country and knows *full well* that before an Act is presented to her by the House of Commons, Parliament has done an *enormous* amount of background research and reading about it and a lot of MPs have spent a lot of time talking about it before it all finally gets written down in old-fashioned writing on traditional House of Commons parchment. In other words, the Monarch is hardly going to suggest chucking it all in the bin, unless she has a real and genuine reason. In fact, Parliament and Monarchy work so closely together nowadays that it is my opinion that Parliament has been made virtually redundant and will *almost certainly be unnecessary* in a couple of years.

A Sensitive Area

The main function of Parliament nowadays is really just to guard against the almost unthinkable event of the Queen suddenly going berserk. Obviously, the idea of our Monarch – beloved as she is across the globe, mother, grandmother, homeopath, patron of the arts – suddenly losing her rag and doing the goose-step and murdering intellectuals is unthinkable, but it is just as well to be on the safe side, as I'm sure she'd be the first to agree. Obviously this is a very delicate and sensitive area and is never actually mentioned. In other words the PM hardly goes up to the Queen and says: 'We're going to have another Parliament this year, in case you go potty'. But it is tacitly understood that that is, in fact, what Parliament is for.

THINGS TO DO

1. Visit the popular Commonwealth landmark: The Commonwealth Institute, in West London, built by Cromwell in 1953. With a wide selection of interesting attractions from the British Commonwealth, such as how to make your own Australian sheep-dip, it is the perfect day-out for the whole family and ideal for kiddies. Unfortunately it was closed in 1989.

2. Visit Commonwealth Way in Plumstead, Commonwealth Road in Tottenham and Commonwealth Avenue near London's famed Wormwood Scrubs.

CHAPTER XXXVIII

The Interregnum

'Oranges are not the only fruit.'
(Nell Gwynn on her death bed)

AFTER King Charles II, who died of too much sexuality with Nell Gwynn, England had a succession of monarchs all of whom caused no trouble at all, I'm happy to say.

Nell Gwynn

William of Orange

The next king was William of Orange who was Nell Gwynn's son of course – hence the name. He then married Queen Mary, who began the tradition of the monarch giving her name to a boat, and for this reason were called William and Mary. Then there was Queen Anne, who gave her name to various tables, George I,

George II, George III, and finally George IV, who was the first British monarch not to wear a wig.

The Queen Mary on the Queen Mary

THINGS TO DO

1. Discover the meaning of interregnum.

CHAPTER XXXIX

The Age of Revolution

'We all of us have life to live and work to do.'
(Charlton Heston)

MEANWHILE, Europe was in turmoil.

Tyrants and Despots

As a result various tyrants and despots (Ivan the Terrible, Ming the Merciless etc.) started taking over all over Europe willy-nilly. Some of them (Frederick the Great, Bob the Builder etc.) did do a few things to benefit their people like introducing bye-laws regarding dogs and putting fountains in parks and so forth but they were really

Despot

only interested in one thing. Going to the hair-dressers and masked balls. For this reason the people, being bowed down in their bondage, had numerous civil wars and French Revolutions, in particular the French Revolution.

Immediately Europe was in turmoil. This was basic-ally because all the revolting countries had copied the

British Commonwealth, done their own Houses of Parliament and abolished the Monarch for good. Which is hardly the point, obviously. The whole point of having a revolution is to abolish the Monarch *for a while.* Till the country gets back on its feet again. And then bring him back. Just like we done with Charles I. In other words, *don't jack the monarchy in for ever!* Otherwise all hell breaks loose, which is exactly what happened, of course, and why the whole of Europe became immediately riven with anarchy,[1] which is what occurs if you don't have a sensible monarch on the throne.

No Buses

In fact, when you have anarchy, there are no buses, trains, postmen or nothing. Everyone just does whatever he feels like doing and basically doesn't care who he offends in the process.

If I was a well-known *anarchist* historian writing this book, for example, my *sole intention* would be to unnecessarily shock and offend my audience, regardless of the consequences. In other words, although this volume might appear to, to all intents and purposes, to be a perfectly normal academic oeuvre, you the reader would know, deep within you, that *at any moment I could simply pull out the rug from under your eyes.*

You'd be approaching the end of the page.

You'd read on as normally as you could.

But all the time you'd have, lurking within you, the terrible knowledge that this is the world of the anarchist where anything can happen! Where the following page might contain material of such an unnecessarily offensive nature that you might never ever see life in the same way

---

1. Anarchy is in fact an ancient Greek word and means literally: *an* = lack of, *archy* = a sensible monarch.

As it happens it didn't.

But it could have.

And that's the point I'm making.

And why so many non-British people, such as the French, for instance, are always in a state of permanent anxiety. They live their lives as best they can. But they know – deep down – that they are *play-acting at normality.* That, at any moment, Dame Anarchy and her three twin sisters, Shock, Outrage and Unnecessary Offence, can come bursting through the paper-thin veneer of their dull and humdrum lives.

And why is this?

Because they've all abolished their monarchs.

It is, in fact, a fascinating and strange irony that apart from Holland and Tonga, Great Britain – who was the very first country in the world to *replace* a monarch – is now the only country in the world that still *has* a monarch!

Unbelievable as this may seen.

Queen of Netherlands

THINGS TO DO

1. Find a monarch of your own and abolish him (or her).

2. Release from bondage an oppressed person of your acquaintance.

CHAPTER XL

The Age of Reason

'You're the reason.'
(Esther and Abi Ofarim)

THE Age of Revolution was also known, of course, as the Age of Reason which it's very important to have as well, obviously, and was chiefly run by Renee Descartes, not to mention Renee Zellweger, who were two of the most reasonable people you could hope to meet. Their philosophy of 'I think therefore I am' became immensely popular but went swiftly out of fashion when it was changed to 'I am therefore I think' by Sir Jack Hobbes the renowned thinker and cricketer.[1] He then changed it to 'I neither am nor think' which confused everybody and finally to 'I don't think I am' which made everyone happier but lead inevitably to the next age, the Age of Turmoil, which is one of the most turbulent ages ever known.

THINGS TO DO

1. Find a good reason.

---

1. And ancestor of the famed philosopher and kettle magnate Sir Russell Hobbes

The Age of Turmoil

'A maun of maids dun is worth ne'er a wink'
(Anon. Meaning obscure)

Fortunately the Age of Turmoil didn't last long other-wise who knows what we'd have done.

THINGS TO DO

1. Explain **one** of the following: **(a)** Turmoil.

The Life of Doctor Johnson

'Doctor Johnson, I presume.'
(Boswell)

ONE of the most famous people to occur at this juncture was, of course, Doctor Johnson, the world-famous man of letters, although, tragically, many of his letters have been lost because the GPO was still in a very rudimentary state, without such things as automated sorting and the post code.

At the same time, contemporary roads were plagued with highwaymen, so that even if a letter didn't get mislaid in a rudimentary sub-post office, it would almost certainly have got stolen en route. Although why a highwayman would want to steal people's letters I have no idea, seeing as most people's letters are extremely dull, particularly if you don't know them.

Dr Johnson

The End of Johnson

In his later years, Dr Johnson gave up private practice to write the classic best-seller Boswell's *Life of Johnson*, and its sequel Johnson's *Life of Boswell*, which he completed shortly before his untimely death in 1931.

Ulrika Johnssson

THINGS TO DO

1. Write Boswell's *Life of Johnson*.

CHAPTER XLIII

World Affairs: 1851

'World affairs was very important at this time."
(Simon Schmrama)

MEANWHILE, the rest of the world more or less carried on as it had been doing and didn't really start changing yet particularly.[1]

---

1. I should just like to take this opportunity to point out that I am fully aware this is meant to be a history of the whole world, thank you Raymond!! And obviously, if I had limitless time I would be perfectly happy to trudge through what all the other countries of the whole world was doing at this time, but it is somewhat difficult when you've also got some nineteen-year-old secretary phoning up every ten minutes saying when can they expect 'the text' (whatever that is) and Mr Herm doesn't understand this and Mr Herm doesn't understand that and is there enough detail in the chapter on the Bronze Age etc. etc. etc! Enough detail!!? The point is that there isn't anything else *known* about the Bronze Age!! Besides which the Bronze Age only lasted a couple of years anyway, so what's all the fuss about! I have no wish to be disrespectful to Mr Herm who, I know, is in his nineties and has gall stones, but he hasn't had to spend weeks and weeks of his life sacrificing sleep and nearly all his leisure pursuits hacking through the history of the world day in day out till he's blue in the face! Alone in his bed-sit. Catching tuberculosis from lack of food. Does he think I enjoy it! So it is NOT HELPFUL RAYMOND having you suddenly jumping on the band wagon and whittling on about the length of certain chapters when, not only is it NOT one of your duties to comment, but you have absolutely no knowledge of the subject anyway! Besides which – and I'm sorry to expose my colleague in this public manner but I feel I have no option – I have been asking Raymond for weeks to unblock the sink in the kitchen. This was so as to remove the awful smell which has been there for literally days now. So far – what has Raymond done? Absolutely nothing! The net result being that, besides writing *The Complete History of the Entire World* totally and

THINGS TO DO

1. You try and write a complete history of the world totally alone and unaided all by yourself.

alone and unaided AND facing a endless battery of unhelpful queries and criticisms from the publisher, I AM NOW FACED WITH HAVING TO UNBLOCK THE SINK MYSELF!!! Seeing as the smell of whatever's in there is so bad that I can barely use the toilet which happens to be through the kitchen as it happens. Does Simon Schramarama unblock his own sinks? I THINK NOT!!! Does Lady Antonia Fraser? Answer: No! Raymond's contract with the National Theatre of Brent, besides doing such things as set building, acting and catering, is to carry out simple household chores, such as unblocking plumbing as and when it arises!!! It certainly isn't to come swanning in and criticizing all and sundry whenever he feels like it! What I'm saying is that it's not that I don't *know* all about all the other countries, it's just that, owing to unforeseen circumstances beyond my control, I simply do not have the *time* to go into every single minuscule detail of every other country unfortunately! But alright, if you want to know what was going on in Japan, for example, which you've just picked at random apparently, then alright, I'll tell you *precisely* what's going on in Japan and I'll ask you to shut up, thank you Raymond.

CHAPTER XLIV

The History of Japan

'So what about Japan then?'
(Raymond Box)

JAPAN had not changed at all basically and was still totally traditional in her traditions and therefore holds very little interest to the modern historian as it happens, Raymond.

Inscrutable

Nevertheless, let us pause a moment to gaze upon this inscrutable land so full of 'eastern promise'.

Japanese People

Japanese people were ruled by Shoguns, who fought numerous wars against other Shoguns, as has been demonstrated in the famous best-seller *Shogun*.

Japanese Customs

Otherwise most Japanese people's time was spent doing tea rituals and miniature gardening.[1] As they do to this day. Besides which they had many other customs, too numerous to go into at this juncture. Obviously customs are very important when you go into a country and when you come out of it, though it can often involve queuing.

---

1. Japanese gardens are usually only about a foot square, due to overcrowding in inner cities.

Conclusion

And so it was that the rising sun did set upon the mighty Japanese empire.

THINGS TO DO

1. Make a model of a friend or relative, using the traditional Japanese craft of paper-folding or *hari-kiri*.

CHAPTER XLV

The Interregnum

'Let them eat cake.'
(Queen Victoria)

AFTER William IV came William V or 'Rufus',[1] then
his son Edward VI, then Edward VII his son, then
his son Edward VIII and finally his grandmother Queen
Victoria – famed, of course, for choosing as her title the
legendary railway station of the same name. St Pancras is
probably more exotic architecturally, but her courtiers
warned her against naming herself Queen Pancras for
medical reasons.

Queen Victoria

Queen Victoria ascended the throne at eighteen with her
husband and consortium, Prince Albert Hall. Together
with some of the greatest Prime Ministers known to man,
her mighty legs bestraddled the peeping world like a
Colossus, bringing light to the starving and bread to them
as grieved without redress.

Honoured for All Time

And the names of those Prime Ministers will be remembered too and honoured for all time. Men who dedicated
their whole lives and sacrificed all, often working late into
the night, to bring a ray of hope to their despairing felows.
Men like Robert Walpole, Pitt the Elder, Pitt the Younger,

---

1. Or Rufus Sewell obviously.

Victoria and Albert

The Old Pretender, The Blue Boy, Neville Chamberlain, Charles de Gaulle, Scott of the Antarctic, and Dame Kiri Te Kanawa.

THINGS TO DO

1. Visit Dame Kiri te Kanawa in:

    (a) her suite at Claridges Hotel, London;

    (b) her personal dressing room at the Royal Opera House;

    (c) her attractive sheep farm in Auckland, New Zealand.

She would be only too delighted to sign your copy of this work.

CHAPTER XLVI

The Napoleonic Wars

'Friendship is a golden chain,
The links are friends so dear
And like a rare and precious jewel
It's treasured more each year.'
(Helen Steiner Rice – *Just for You*)

The Napoleonic Wars

These were fought at approximately this time and were begun by Napoleon, as the name implies.

The End of the Napoleonic Wars

Almost immediately the end of the Napoleonic Wars occurred at the Battle of Trafalgar Square, which was won, of course, by the Admiral Lord Nelson, who was famous for losing an eye and an arm and being killed at the same time.

The Results of the Napoleonic Wars

As a result of the Napoleonic Wars, Napoleon was exiled to Corfu, where he was also born, of course, and where he now returned to live with his ageing grandparents. They tried to interest him in some tropical fish and a home wine-making kit but such pursuits held little joy for one who had wielded such power as he had done. Immediately he could bear it no more and escaped, disguised as a washerwoman, meeting the English at the famous Battle of Waterloo in South London. But his old powers were waning. He had lost his hair, besides which his right hand had mysteriously vanished. For this reason,

Napoleon

the battle was won by the Duke of Wellington, the legendary Duke. Wellington returned to a hero's welcome and immediately asked for a column like Nelson's and a square. But the Arts Council had nothing left in its non-regional budget so he had to settle for Waterloo Station, which isn't bad, seeing as it serves nearly the whole of the south of England. Provided the trains are running, obviously.

THINGS TO DO

1. Decide which of the following is the most likely place for Napoleon to have lost his hand:

- **(a)** The Eiffel Tower;

- **(b)** The guillotine;

- **(c)** Madame Tussauds.

★ ★ ★

LITTLE-KNOWN THEORIES NO. I

There is a rather intriguing theory that is currently gaining some credence in historical circles and is my own theory, as it happens, namely that Nelson and Napoleon were in fact one and the same person, owing to the similarity in names and hats and the fact that they both only had the one hand. The only hole in this theory is how one man could have been both Nelson and Napoleon in the Battle of Trafalgar Square without anyone else knowing, i.e. how he could have got from one flagship to the other, changed costumes, had himself killed as Nelson, nipped back to being Napoleon again, then back to being Nelson to have himself buried at sea and then back in time for Napoleon's victory parade in Paris? Unfortunately, there is no easy answer to this fascinating historical riddle. Suffice it to say, in the immortal dying words of Sir Thomas Hardy: 'There's more to this than meets the eye in my opinion'.

CHAPTER XLVII

The American War of Independence

'Yanky doodle, keep it up
Yanky doodle dandy.'
(American National Anthem)

AMERICA, of course, was still being run by the British
Government at this time so a number of people decided to start the famous American War of Independence.
As a result the British Government sent the entire British
army – or 'Red Coats'[1] – under Lord Butcher Cumberland,
the well-known unpopular general. They had numerous
battles, particularly the Boston Tea-Party, the Gettysburg

Butcher Cumberland

1. See notes on Butlin's, page 83.

Address and the Battle of the Bulge, but the Confederates or Yankee Doodles, as they was known, being more conversant with the terrain and not having the red coats obviously, won.

For this reason, America became independent and had the Declaration of Independence under George Washington, which meant they were now American and not British, but would obviously always admire Britain a great deal. They also agreed to give thanks to Britain for her many years of wise and beneficial Government, and decided therefore to have a special day each year to mark their gratitude which would be called 'Thanksgiving Day'. In other words a special day to thank Britain for all its help in getting America off the ground, so to speak, which is, in fact, their equivalent of our Christmas Day, when everybody has turkey and presents and crackers.

For this reason, and it's hardly surprising when you think about it, the Americans decided to run the country very much on British lines, which they do to this day except they don't have a Monarch but a President, who lives more like a Monarch than a Monarch, if you ask me, judging by the size of the White House and the vast number of rooms in it.[1] Unlike our own PM who lives very humbly indeed in Number 10 Downing Street with all his family and a massive staff in only two bedrooms.

THINGS TO DO

1. Fight a War of Independence from anyone of your choice.

2. Hold a Boston tea party.

3. Build a White House.

---

1. A point also made by many world-famous leading historians, in particular Sir Simon Schrmarama and Dame Antonia Fraser.

CHAPTER XLVIII

The Nineteenth Century

'But facts are chiels that winna ding.'
(Burns)

THE nineteenth century occurred straight after the American War of Independence and is chiefly remembered for The Industrial Revolution which suddenly broke out at this time.

Reasons Behind the Industrial Revolution

The reasons behind the Industrial Revolution was mainly all the numerous inventions that started being made by various inventors at this time, such as Crompton's Mule by James Arkwright; Arkwright's Mule by James Crompton; Stevenson's Rocket by James Herriot; Wordsworth's Prelude by Robert Louis Stevenson; and the Electric Kettle by Watt Tyler. Not to mention Constable's Haywain, Thompson's Gazelle, the *Reader's Digest* and Scott's Porridge Oats. All of which were discovered during this momentous age. Needless to say, however, it wasn't all a bunch of bluebells.

Before the Industrial Revolution

Before the Industrial Revolution, virtually the whole country lived in the country, generally in Dorset, and spent their lives clog-dancing, sheep-dipping, making haystacks, and selling home-made doylies.[1]

---

1. From the French *de oylé: de* = for prevention of; *oylé* = unsightly grease. Doylies were introduced in rural communities to prevent

Stevenson's Rocket

The Industrial Revolution

Suddenly, however, the Industrial Revolution occurred and within days factories and coalmines started going up all over Europe. Immediately tiny little ponies were shipped down from the Shetlands to drag massively heavy iron barges full of granite rocks the entire length of the Manchester Ship Canal while starving children with scurvy and malaria were forced up chimneys the second they were out of nappies or dragooned into hauling huge railway trucks laden with massive ton weights of coal uphill for miles through pitch-black airless rat-infested winding tunnels prone to collapse at any minute. A tradition still carried on in many Yorkshire pits to this day.

Shopping

The Industrial Revolution is also responsible of course for the discovery of shopping which was almost unknown until the early twentieth century. As a result, many leading High Street stores first appeared at this time, including Marks

butter dripping off muffins on to the furniture, which, of course, was all antique and therefore costly to clean.

and Spencers,[1] W.H. Smith, Dixons, Etam and Miss Selfridge.

The End of the Nineteenth Century

And thus it was that the sun set on the mighty nineteenth century.

THINGS TO DO

1. Construct this simple *1892 Parsons Radial Flow Steam Turbine Engine* (*see illus. overleaf*) – the first steam turbine to surpass in efficiency a reciprocated engine of equal output.

1. Many of whose products are still renowned to this day, including prawn-flavoured petals and male underpants which have revolution-ized men's private areas the world over.

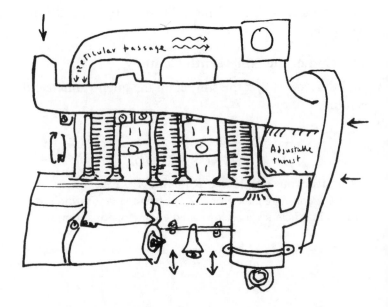

1892 The Parsons Radial Flow Steam Turbine Engine.

INSTRUCTIONS FOR USE

The steam enters through a double governor valve and then flows radially from the centre to the circumference of six wheels, arranged in series with concentric rows of blading, alternating with fixed rows on the diaphragms. The steam then passes from one to the next by reticular passages formed in the diaphragms. The longitudinal pressure exerted on the turbine shafts is counterbalanced by a grooved piston at the HP end of the shaft, excess pressure being taken by the adjustable thrust block which locates the rotor. Don't forget the flexible coupling to the alternator shaft.

CHAPTER XLIX

The Vote

'Hoc erat in votis. Modus agri non ita magnus.
Hortus ubi et tecto vicinus jugis aquae fons
Et palum silvae super his foret. Auctius atque
Di melius fecere. Bene est.'
[It's very important everyone has the vote
in my opinion.]
(Horace) [1]

ANYWAY, as soon as word reached Queen Victoria and the Government's ears about all the kiddies and ponies being shoved up chimneys, they immediately commenced doing numerous reforms, particularly in regarding the Vote, which is a crucial feature of a democracy such as ours and without which society would collapse immediately.

The Vote

Up until this time, of course, only the nobility had the vote, which means that out of a population of three hundred and twenty-nine million there was a total electorate of fifty-three so that election results tended to be a somewhat foregone conclusion.

On Polling Day, the nobles would arrive in their carriages, have a glass of champagne with the candidate, put their cross on the card, have another glass of champagne with the candidate and gallop off to a point-to-

---

1. The popular Greek poet. Surname unknown.

point in Shipton-under-Wychwood. Minutes later, the Election Results would be announced by a tiny black boy in blue satin with a white wig.

Here is a result typical of the time:

Con	52
Ind	0
Lab	0
Ecol	0
Lib Dem	1

The Jarrow March

This obviously was not overly popular with the rest of the population who, for this reason, had the famous Jarrow March. And as they marched, people even poorer than themselves came out of their houses and gave them mugs of tea, boots, biscuits and lard as they camped beside The Great North Road and the nobles' carriages splashed by and they sang together, songs of the dignity of man, beneath the slow-turning starry sky.

And so it was they met the Queen. On a cold and wintry Christmas Eve. And she rode out alone on her horse, Black Beauty, to meet them on Wimbledon Common and a huge hush went over the massive crowd and she spoke gently to their leaders, Jack Cade and Dorothy Perkins, and assured them that everyone would have the vote from hereon in; and that all factories would be pulled down; and no one would catch bronchitis down the mines no more; and that everything would be made by robots; and everyone would have an equal share of the gigantic profit; and live in little thatched cottages and be totally self-sufficient and swap vegetables and play reed-flutes and write poems and children would roam and skip in the sun-dappled forests and green-carpeted English hills and have no disease for evermore.

This was obviously not actually possible, owing to the fact that the British Government had already spent millions of pounds on various crucial things like the Indian Mutiny, the Zulu Wars, the Charge of the Light Brigade and the Ideal Home Exhibition. But, obviously, Queen Victoria couldn't be expected to know all that, seeing as money is a very very complicated business, as any financial expert will tell you. Particularly for a busy monarch.

All the same, she spoke to the marchers gently and with understanding and courteously answered their queries. Then, after she had gone home to a roaring fire and family Christmas at Balmoral, they were beaten up by mounted police with long staves who charged them down where they stood so they wouldn't do it again.

And they lay shivering all night on the frozen ground and most of them died. Including little children. Then they went home to Jarrow.

The Vote

And all the factories carried on churning out identical tumblers and grey lino until Lord Melbourne, the great Australian Prime Minister, saw how depressing all the products were and persuaded the Government to let everyone have a vote finally, which meant that everyone could vote for who they wanted which meant that not surprisingly the Conservatives took a bit of a tumble, seeing as their main election platform was the abolition of admission charges to gymkhanas and the injection of all workers with compulsory rickets.

The Whigs

As a result the Whig Party swept to power on the platform of free wigs for all. This was hardly surprising, seeing as the cost of wigs at the time was extortionate and failure to wear an adequate toupée or hairpiece punishable by hanging. The Conservatives retaliated, by offering

Lord Melbourne

everyone free dinners and their own time-share villa in the Seychelles. So the Whigs changed their name to Labour and offered to send the Conservatives to Australia and give everyone free groceries for life. So the Conservatives changed their name to Tories and offered the entire population £500,000 each and the abolition of all Income Tax (including arrears). Then Prince Albert died, and Queen Victoria – who was just about to step in and put an end to all this vote-catching nonsense – went delirious and abolished sex. Which went on for the next seventy years until she died in 1938.

The Emaciation of Women

This period was also very important for the emaciation of women. Many of whom were outraged at the fact that only men got the vote and they weren't allowed to, which is absurd, obviously, seeing as women are human beings the same as everyone else. The leader of the women in their struggle for emaciation was the famous majorette, Mrs Pankhurst, who chained herself to Buckingham Palace and committed numerous other atrocities on herself to bring the plight of women to the attention of the Queen, who was a woman, after all, but who had unfortunately gone berserk, owing to Albert having died, and ordered Mrs Pankhurst lashed to two sets of frenzied stallions galloping in opposite directions.

Emaciating Women

Alfred the Great

Fortunately this particular form of punishment had been repealed by Alfred the Great, so she was given a life sentence in Dartmoor, suspended for six thousand years. Undeterred, women led marches, held conferences, wore trousers, had women-only dances, became bus conductors and sat in circles with the moon painted on their brows. All of which had a profound effect on men who started breaking down in the street, going into psychoanalysis and weeping openly for no apparent reason.

This is known as the birth of feminism. And, speaking as a feminist – seeing as I am regarded as a feminist by many very feminist women – I would like to say that I believe that women still deserve full emaciation and I – along with many women – will not rest until this day has been achieved.

New Discoveries

At the same time, many English people were discovering large areas of the known world, such as Dr Livingstone, who discovered Africa and Stanley, who discovered Dr Livingstone.

The Historic Meeting of Stanley and Livingstone.
One of the most legendary meetings of all time.

Meanwhile China was discovered by Marco Polo and Australia by Thomas Cook and Son.

THINGS TO DO

1. Write an endless nineteenth-century novel.

2. Visit the following famous nineteenth-century landmarks: Shipton-under-Wychwood, Piccadilly Circus, the Arts Council of Great Britain, Australia.

CHAPTER L

The Twentieth Century

'Everything is becoming Hamlet.'
(Sir Peter Hall – *The Secret Diary of Peter Hall*)

MEANWHILE, Europe was once again in turmoil, owing to a number of reasons.

The Russian Revolution

In Russia, the Czar and Czarina fell under the sinister thrall of the horribly bearded mad monk Rasputin and as a result spent the entire Russian budget buying him presents and having orgies in the Kremlin. For this reason, the Russian peasants, who had lived on a diet of their own shoes for the last nine hundred years, had the Russian Revolution, which is hardly surprising.

The First World War

Meanwhile, in Germany, Kaiser 'Bill' II and the Bismarck started the First World War which they lost, fortunately.

The Roaring Twenties

After which was the Roaring Twenties, famous for the Charleston[1] and the Thirties, which were very depressing.

The Second World War

These were then followed by the Second World War, which was started by the Germans once again, I'm sorry to say, and won, of course, by the English.

---

1. A rather interesting amalgam of the names Charlton and Heston which as yet appears to have been noticed only by myself.

Rasputin – the famed mad monk

1945

1945 was probably the most crucial year in the history of the Earth, besides which it was also a crucial year in my own life, as it happens. This is because it was – remarkably – the *year that I was born.*

I say 'remarkably', because people are always staggered when they hear this, having usually made the assumption from my photographs (see the plates in this volume, for instance) and my theatrical, television and radio appearances that I am considerably younger. Usually in my early thirties.

However – astounding as it may seem – I was truly born in 1945.

The Birth of Desmond Olivier Dingle

In fact, and not many people know this, I actually made my 'first appearance' as it were to the actual sounds of the Bells of Victory themselves. As the first great cry of 'Freedom' echoed across the nations. (And, new-born infant though I was, how will I forget that sound?)

For, believe it or not, I *was born at the stroke of midnight on the very last day of World War II.* My mother – Mrs Evadne Dingle – going into labour actually during those last darkest hours. As the peace of the world teetered in the balance and she strode through the Blitz with her tea and biscuits, helping the needy, encouraging the destitute and defusing unexploded bombs, before finally hearkening to the pleas of those thousands of East Enders, whom she was at that moment personally helping to drag from the rubble of their homes, who begged her to look to herself and her as yet unborn foetus.

And so – the Battle of Britain raging about her – she finally reached Piccadilly Tube air-raid shelter, in the heart of London's East End. And lo! There it was that I was born, a breech delivery as it happens,[1] in the cramped privacy of a London Transport junction box, because there was no room for her on the platform. And still it moves me to think of her, bearing my little unborn self through those last desperate months of wartime, with only one boiled potato, three onions and a spoonful of powdered egg to sustain her and yet thinking never of herself but only of others in their need.

My Guilt

Little did she know, of course, that to have spared her her ante-natal discomfort and to have had the chance, however brief, to assist in the War Effort myself, I would willingly have been born many months premature. As it happens, I was born three months late, her labour lasted sixteen weeks and I weighed four and a half stone at birth. Something I have never forgiven myself for. And just one of the many personal burdens I still carry to this day.

An Uncanny Coincidence

An uncanny coincidence is that a number of theatrical celebrities was also born in 1945, including – believe it or not – the Artistic Director of the Royal National Theatre Sir Trevor Nunn and not only him but also his previous incumbent the renowned director and theatre expert Sir

---

1. And one of the most difficult and most dangerous births there is, of course. Particularly in the Underground.

Sir Trevor Nunn

Richard Eyres. And – even *more* extraordinary – that the new Artistic Director Sir Nicholas Hytner (and an excellent choice if I may but drop in my humble penn'orth)[1] was born in that year also!

Further proof, if any were needed, that our lives are not our own 'but written upon the stars'.

THINGS TO DO

1. Describe in your own words your own birth.

2. Plan an orgy with Rasputin.

---

1. Needless to say I was disappointed and not a little hurt when I heard that the Royal National Theatre board had finally gone for him as opposed to myself in the role of Artistic Supremo of the National Theatre. But I should like to make it absolutely clear that I bear him no hard feelings whatsoever. In fact I have taken it upon myself to offer him my personal services in an advisory capacity, terms to be negotiated, obviously.

CHAPTER LI

The Fifties

'And thence came the fifties.'
(Anon)

THEN after the War came the fifties, when everything was rebuilt, such as the slums.

The fifties was also famous for the Coronation, the ascent of Everest, the discovery of ITV, Wimbledon, and the construction of the Suez Canal by Cecil Rhodes. This vastly reduced the length of boat trips to Australia but came as a deep shock to the Egyptians who had no idea he was doing it. It therefore became known as the Suez Crisis and severely rocked the Tory Government who for this reason introduced prescription charges and inflation.

THINGS TO DO

1. Ascend Everest.

CHAPTER LII

The Sixties

Но на чужо́й мане́р хлеб ру́сский не роди́тся
(Nikita Krushchev)

THE sixties was famous for youth, chiefly, who became particularly numerous at this time. This was
mainly as a result of the world-famous popular singing
duo, The Beatles, who was prodigiously successful and
done numerous hit records, for instance, 'I Can't Get No
Satisfaction' and 'Hound Dog'. For this reason, they became household names and modern youth rebelled against
their parents causing havoc across the world. Besides many
things, The Beatles also started hippies, who became the
latest craze for many years, and contraceptives.

The Space Race

Also in the sixties, the space race began and the Russians
put the first living creature in space, the famous Russian
dog pilot, Potemkin, who, although he successfully piloted
a Sputnik round the earth for seven and a half months
and was able to report his progress with a series of barks,
returned home appallingly thin and neurotic, seeing as,
before him, no-one realized that space has no gravity
so he spent the entire journey floating upside down and
unable to reach the tubes containing his dinner (*see artist's
reconstruction*).

On subsequent journeys, doggie cosmonauts Rusky
and Chekhov were given special suction footpads and a
unique automatic 'walkies' belt that operated continually

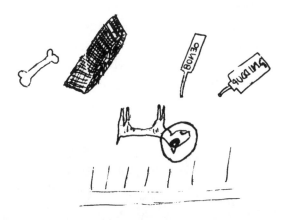

The Tragic Journey of Potemkin (artist's reconstruction)

through the flight, only stopping for food and sleep at four-hour intervals. The only tragedy occurred during the flight of Rusky – when the automatic pilot, PAL 2000, went berserk, turned off the central heating and force-fed her for four hours at a time without any walkies. She splashed down in the Black Sea totally unslept, horribly obese and frozen to her basket.

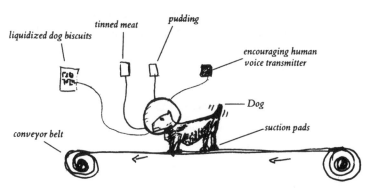

The Flight of Rusky

The Profumo Affair

Refers to the famous affair between Christine Keeler and the well-known MP Lord Profumo who, being Italian, tended to be somewhat volatile when it come to his proclivities. Unfortunately, this story has been much sensationalized so I have no wish to go into it in any further detail.

The Profumo Affair

Suffice to say it involved various goings on with a bevy of scantily-clad nymphettes and most of the Tory Party. Not to mention the House of Lords, the BBC and the Russians.

Once again this severely rocked the Tory Government who therefore doubled prescription charges, joined the Common Market and introduced VAT.

THINGS TO DO

1. Make a scale model of Twiggy.

CHAPTER LIII

The Seventies

'Many a mickle makes a muckle.'
(Richard Nixon)

THE seventies was chiefly famous for Watergate and numerous technological advances such as Concorde and Music Centres when you had the radio, tape and record in one thing.

THINGS TO DO

Either 1. Write an essay entitled 'Who would I rather be if I had the choice, the Bay City Rollers, the Bee Gees or Richard Nixon?' Give your reasons.

Or 2. Re-write 'Chirpie Chirpie Cheep Cheep' in your own words.

CHAPTER LIV

The Eighties

'We blossom and flourish as leaves on the tree,
And wither and perish but nought changeth thee.'
(Judith Chalmers)

THE eighties was famous, of course, for videos, Mrs Thatcher and 1984, based on the popular novel of the same name.

THINGS TO DO

1. Write *1984*.

CHAPTER LV

The Nineties

'*We live and learn but not the wiser grow.*'
(Desmond Olivier Dingle)

THE nineties came in immediately after the eighties. It was famous for mobile phones and celebrity weddings, such as Becks and Spice, which cost millions of pounds and was watched by over twice the population of the entire world, and Anthea Turner who sold her soul for a flake. Also in the nineties apartheid collapsed and communism collapsed and them who had been enemies embraced on the rubble of broken walls and said now all will be well. Then they had the Millennium.

THINGS TO DO

1. Have a celebrity wedding.

CHAPTER LVI

The Twenty-first Century

'Look before you leap.'
(Mao Tse Tung)

The Twenty-first Century started well with some spectacular fireworks particularly in Sydney though unfortunately it is not looking too promising at the moment to be honest.

THINGS TO DO

Live in Australia.

CHAPTER LVII

The Future

*'The thing that gave me most joy was this.
I was walking across the reception rooms
when I heard a voice crying "Cuckoo".
It was Princess Margaret.'*
(Sir Peter Hall – *The Secret Diary of Peter Hall*)

BUT let us not end this mighty oeuvre – hand-drawn like jewels from the storm-racked ocean of my soul and penned into the early hours of many mornings – on a despairing note.

For I should like to tell you of a dream I had, but a few nights ago, as I lay tossing and turning on my unslept-on bed, wrestling with numerous problems of a personal and global nature. And in the dream I was taken to a field in the dead of night and the clouds parted and there was a noise such as I'd never heard before and a massive UFO landed all covered in lights in the middle of the field and after doing loads of crop circles its silver doors opened and I was invited inside and taken up many miles above the Earth and shown all the stars and planets in the universe and everything in the whole world.

And straight way a small door did open and an extra-terrestrial being appeared with a big head and little arms and a light that come from the pores of his skin and he did tell unto me that I had been specially chosen out of a number of contestants to be a message-bearer to my fellow-earthlings – that lo even though things look somewhat grim at the moment there will come forth a time of light when a mighty still voice will speak and open the door on the silence of everyone's still-most core and lo the little cosmic wanderer on which we have our home will spin her colours across the universe and peace will fall upon her always like the radiant light of the morning. Which is a bit of luck, obviously.

So I said unto the extra-terrestrial with the big head: "But when might this radiant light occur, O extra-terrestrial, seeing as it would be helpful to know at this juncture."

And he did reply unto me various mystic words but immediately I fell into a deep sleep and when I awoke only this tantalising fragment remained.

> 'Do not despair, that you cannot change
> The world in a day or two,
> Instead, just give your very best
> In the little things you do.'

And so I awoke and immediately felt a great and inexplicable joy, a joy so powerful that I could not restrain it but had to burst immediately into song, right where I lay on my unslept-on bed.

In other words, it is my humble belief that I, Desmond Olivier Dingle, have now become an extra-terrestrial message-bearer identical (but for my earthly shape obviously which I shall retain so as not to alarm my fellow earthlings) to the extra-terrestrial with the big head.

Raymond says I have a kind of purple emanation that starts glowing round me at meal times but that's either his imagination or he's just trying to knuckle in. Seeing as the only way Raymond could spot this would be if *he* was an extra-terrestrial message-bearer too, which is impossible, obviously, seeing as the Sentinels of the Universe, with all due respect, would hardly make *Raymond* an extra-terrestrial message-bearer – endowed with the massive responsibility of leading the entire human race into the golden dawn of peace, harmony and eternal sunlight. Not unless they wanted their heads examining.

Now, of course, he's saying he has a purple light around *him* that I can't see – which is absurd, obviously. In fact Raymond would do well to remember that it was *me* who had the mystic dream and not him. Besides which, they'd hardly have *two* extra-terrestrial message-bearers in the Greater London area, would they? If Raymond had been made an extra-terrestrial message-bearer, they'd have put him in Malaysia or somewhere. Which is probably the best place for him in my opinion.

THINGS TO DO

1. Make a crop circle on someone's field.

CHAPTER LVIII

Postlude

'We are all in the gutter but looking at the stars.'
(Oscar Wilde)

AND thus at last the sun does set upon this mighty history of the world. And on all the mighty doings of the men and women gone before. We can picture them now gazing down and wondering, I shouldn't wonder, if it was all worth while and what on earth's going to happen to be honest.

Let us remember them as we spin on in space and hope that all their trials was not in vain.

And hope that when the sun arises in the morning, the history that they done was but the beginning of the history of tomorrow.

THINGS TO DO

1. Give this book to a friend as a stylish and lasting gift that will be treasured for years to come (including a *free leaflet* describing a host of exciting ways to display it in the home). Just simply fill in the exciting form on page 186 and return to Marketing Dept, Nick Herm Books, The Glasshouse, 49a Goldhawk Road, London W12 8QP.

2. Visit the fabulous National Theatre of Brent Website. See page 185 for full details.

3. Precis this entire book in not less than fifteen words.

THE END

Index

The National Theatre of Brent Website

YES!!! You can now visit the National Theatre of Brent on our *VERY OWN WEBSITE*:

Nationaltheatreofbrent.com

Using the very latest in inter-global interweb macrobiotic cybertechnology on a scale virtually unparalleled probably on any of today's modern virtual global highways, we are delighted to transport you to the real yet astonishingly virtual world of our very own website!!!

Here's just a few of the fascinating things you'll be able to do when you 'drop in':

- *Meet me and my entire company – Raymond Box – on a highly personal and intimate basis!*

- *Discover our meteoric Rise to Fame as it happened before your very eyes!*

- *Visit our Problem Page! History questions, theatrical queries, personal problems a speciality. All dealt with in strict confidence!*

- *Discover an whole host of fascinating and totally unexpurgated 'backstage stories'!*

- *Numerous candid photos and interviews with all leading personnel!*

- *Enter our fascinating virtual world simply at the push of a button!*

Nationaltheatreofbrent.com

YES PLEASE, NICK HERM BOOKS!

PLEASE **RUSH** *a copy of* **DESMOND DINGLE'S COMPLETE HISTORY OF THE WHOLE WORLD** *to*

. . . .

Address . . . .

. . . .

as a surprise gift that I believe he/she★ and their children will treasure for the rest of their lives.

TOGETHER WITH a *free* two-colour leaflet (subject to availability) describing a host of exciting ways to display it in the home.

CHOOSE YOUR BINDING AND TICK WHERE APPLICABLE

The 'Classic'   £9.99 (plus p & p)

The 'Renaissance'
(including simulated Medieval Bookmark)
                                   £120.00 (plus p & p)

The 'Babylonian'
(including Medieval Bookmark, replica
Viking Bookstand and Author's Signature.
Limited to 500 only)   £2000.00 (p & p extra)

★ *Delete where necessary*